Beyond
The Veil

Beyond The Veil

by Lee Nelson

Volume One

ISBN: 01-55517-016

Cedar Fort, Inc.
Orem, UT

Lithographed in the United States of America

Dedication

To our friends beyond the veil

Publisher's Foreword

There are two main fears that seem to override all others when a project of this nature is attempted; first, the fear of not being believed; and second, the fear that others will esteem the project as simply commercial.

The accounts in this volume are extremely personal and private. Most persons who have had an experience of this kind are at least reticent to tell it. Nearly all feel they would like to control the opportunities to expose their stories and feelings. In the end, however, the urge to help others—which is usually heightened by their experience—overrides the individual's reluctance.

These narratives are not meant to be read and discussed from a doctrinal point of view, but used simply for whatever benefit may be individually appropriate. The publisher asks specifically that these stories not be passed on orally from friend to friend but only read and pondered in private in order to avoid any distortion or inclination to sensationalize.

Table of Contents

Introduction

When Raymond Moody, author of the best-selling book, *Life After Life,* spoke at a forum assembly at Brigham Young University in Provo, Utah, he said he was amazed at the large number of out-of-body experiences originating in Utah. Though Moody investigated 150 such experiences in writing his book, what he probably didn't realize at the time was that he had barely scratched the surface of a huge reservoir of beyond-the-veil experiences by LDS people who live not only in Utah but all over the world.

Pollster George Gallup, Jr. recently found that an estimated eight million Americans have experienced some sort of mystical encounter in conjunction with a near-death experience. Dr. Michael Sabom, a cardiologist at the Atlanta V.A. Medical Center in Georgia, reported that of 116 patients who suffered near-fatal medical crises, nearly half—43%—reported some kind of supernatural, near-death experience.

Sabom also reported that those who reported leaving their bodies could give amazingly accurate accounts of what medical personnel were doing to their bodies, where doctors and nurses were standing, what the readings were on various monitoring devices, when electric shock treatments were applied, descriptions of operating procedures which the natural body could not possibly have witnessed, even exact recountings of conversations between doctors on their golf games. As a test Sabom asked twenty three long-time heart patients who did not claim any unusual experiences to describe operating room procedures. Twenty made serious errors. Only those who claimed out-of-body experiences could describe accurately and precisely what was going on in the operating room.

This book publishes to the world a new body of after-life experiences, mostly by Mormons. This book adds new testimony—by ordinary people who have been beyond the veil and returned—that the human soul is not snuffed out by death. This is important because—to a large degree—how we view death determines how we live life. Such experiences also give comfort and confidence to those who have lost someone to death or who are facing death themselves.

My fascination with the world beyond the veil began long before this book was begun, even long before Moody's book was published.

I'll never forget my visit to a little, white-haired Mormon patriarch in Heilbron, Germany, in the spring of 1964. I was a missionary in Germany at the time and, as a result of some earnest conversation with a companion, had requested an opportunity to receive a patriarchal blessing. My companion and I rode to Heilbron on the train; then from the station we walked to the home of Emil Geist, patriarch for the Stuttgart Stake. His home was typically German, an apartment in a brown high-rise building at the top of a spotless hand-scrubbed staircase. The only thing I remember about the inside of the apartment was the ceiling which was painted bright red, in sharp contrast to more traditional browns and grays.

Patriarch Geist was a short man, with hair as white as new snow. I guessed his age to be in the mid-70s. We had never met, though I had seen him sitting on the stand at stake conference. To him, at first impression, I was no different than any of the other 200 American-born missionaries serving in Southern Germany at the time. He had never seen me before I appeared at his door and would probably never see me again, at least not on this side of the veil.

No one told him that before my mission I was a college student majoring in physics, that I had no particular interest in English or writing. With the confidence of an Old Testament prophet he laid his hands on my head and, as part of the blessing, told me that through my words I would find great success in life, both inside and outside the Church, that the Lord would put words in my mouth that would be of great value to my fellow men, that through my words I would strengthen the poor, the weak and the lazy, and that through my words I would be blessed in great abundance with the things of this world. Of course, the blessing was in German; he didn't speak English.

As I left Patriarch Geist's home that day I knew I was going to be a writer. This field of endeavor had never interested me before, I suppose because up until that point in time, I didn't think I was very good at it. Upon returning to the United States I changed my college major from physics to English, became a public relations writer, a speech writer, an advertising copywriter, eventually getting into feature articles and books (fourteen completed and more in process). Every time I finish a book I give quiet thanks to that little German patriarch, a total stranger, who had the spiritual confidence to lay his hands on my head and point my life in a new direction.

With this as background material presented in the hope that you, the reader, might share some of the same confidence in this patriarch that I have, I will now tell you something else he said in that blessing, something that ties in closely with the subject of this book.

He said I would win friends on the other side of the veil, and in turn, those friends would help me in this life through the means available to them. He didn't specify what those means were, but ever since that moment, in times of crisis, I have looked over my shoulder wondering what spirit presence might be getting ready to lend a helping hand.

I have never heard a voice or seen a face, but on several occasions when in serious physical danger, I have sensed helping hands from beyond the veil: like the time in California when I was sliding off a ledge into a vertical mine shaft, and I suddenly stopped with no rational explanation, though the surface to which I had been trying to cling had become steeper; like the time on the Salt Lake freeway when a tanker truck turned into my little station wagon at 60 miles per hour, sending the car into a spin in heavy traffic. All four sides of the car were crushed, three windows smashed, both seat backs broken. Three members of my family were with me. By the time the spinning car came to a halt, we were covered with broken glass, but not one of us received a scratch.

I have often wished I could communicate with my friends on the other side of the veil. I have been reluctant to get involved with seances, channeling, and that sort of thing in an effort to avoid possible contact with evil spirits. Still, I have had a strong desire over the years to know more about my friends beyond the veil who Patriarch Geist promised would be trying to help me. Who are these friends? When do they come around? How do they help? Can they read my thoughts? What would they say to me if I could hear them? Are they male or female? Had I known them in the flesh? Are they my relatives? These questions continue to haunt me. With this background, you, the reader, can appreciate my immediate interest when Lyle Mortimer of Cedar Fort, Inc. called in the spring of 1988, asking if I wanted to help him put together this book. By studying other people's experiences beyond the veil, I would gain a better understanding and appreciation of my own friends beyond the veil. Maybe I would learn something that would enable me to have better affinity with them.

Lyle explained that he had already gathered some stories that would be appropriate for such a book and that he would continue to gather material as I was writing the book. Of course, I would be looking for stories myself. My purpose in compiling the stories would be to apply my writing skills to make them clear and readable, but not to embellish or glamourize. My objective was to capture in words, as accurately as possible, what the person who had the experience was trying to convey. One of my concerns in accepting the assignment was how difficult it might be to find enough good material to justify a book. Those fears were quickly forgotten. I picked up two potential stories in a brief conversation at a high school soccer game. I found three more in my own neighborhood. When I mentioned the subject of the book to a doctor friend, he spent an hour relating beyond-the-veil experiences he had come across in practicing medicine. He mentioned the name of another doctor who could tell me many more. That's when I realized that even though Moody had studied 150 life-after-life experiences for his book, he had only scratched the surface, at least in the Mormon community. In fact, I am convinced that I could go into nearly any stake in the Church and find numerous beyond the veil experiences suitable for publication. As I began the project, I cautioned my wife that she shouldn't be too alarmed should I die. I told her I was praying for my own beyond-the-veil experience, and if my request were granted, she should not become too alarmed. She should just hold off the undertaker, allowing me time to return. At press time, that prayer has not yet been answered.

Anyone doubting there could be so many legitimate beyond-the-veil experiences should read from Moroni 7 in the Book of Mormon. Beginning at the end of verse 35 we read:

"Has the day of miracles ceased?

"Or have angels ceased to appear unto the children of men? Or has he withheld the power of the Holy Ghost from them? Or will he, so long as time shall last, or the earth shall stand, or there shall be one man upon the face thereof to be saved?

"Behold I say unto you, Nay; for it is by faith that miracles are wrought; and it is by faith that angels appear and minister unto men; wherefore, if these things have ceased wo be unto the children of men, for it is because of unbelief, and all is vain.

"For no man can be saved, according to the words of Christ, save they shall have faith in his name; wherefore, if these things have ceased, then has faith ceased also; and awful is the state of man, for they are as though there had been no redemption made."

Or if anyone should question the appropriateness of retelling or studying these experiences remember Joseph Smith's statement:

"All men know that they must die. . . . It is but reasonable to suppose that God would reveal something in reference to the matter, and it is a subject we ought to study more than any other. . . . If we have any claim on our Heavenly Father for anything, it is for knowledge on this important subject."

Some of the people we contacted did not want their stories published. Some felt their experiences were too sacred to be published for just anybody to read. Others felt that while their stories were sacred too, they wanted them published so those reading this book could share the strength and comfort found in the stories. Some asked that their names be withheld.

All but one of the experiences related in this book are told by Mormons. The one exception is a story by Arthur Ford. This account was included so readers not familiar with the works of Moody and others could see the remarkable similarities between a non-Mormon beyond-the-veil experience and those experienced by Latter-day Saints.

I might add that not all the stories in this volume are about people from this world passing beyond the veil. Some are about spirit persons from the other side coming to this side of the veil. In all the stories, the veil—the barrier between this life and the spirit world—is crossed.

After reviewing numerous beyond-the-veil experiences, many of which were not published in this book for various reasons, some common elements seem to surface. If a model or typical example could be created, it would go something like this. At the ultimate point in pain or agony, the subject suddenly finds himself separated from his body, usually in the air above the body looking down. He can see the doctors or attendants frantically trying to revive the body, or he can hear them pronouncing the body dead—but they cannot see or hear him. He finds he still has a body, but it is different, consisting of a finer spirit matter. He can pass through walls or other physical objects.

He is greeted by a spirit person or escort, usually clad in white. They travel through a tunnel or valley. Often the subject is alone when traveling through the tunnel. Some cannot remember a tunnel. If color is mentioned, it might be green.

The subject then approaches some sort of barrier, like a door or large room, where frequently he is greeted by former acquaintances who have died. These individuals do not have wings, normally do not sing in choirs but seem busily engaged in important work.

Sometimes the subject gets a glimpse of another part of the spirit world where spirits are not happy. Sometimes scenes from the subject's life are flashed before him, a heavenly version of instant replay. There is an intense feeling of love, joy and peace in a world where time is not measured. Often communication takes place without words, the subject and those about him communicating with thought only, like they are reading each other's minds.

When the subject is informed that his time to die has not yet arrived, that he must return to his physical body, there is usually reluctance to go back. When the spirit re-enters the body the former pain and suffering returns. As a result of the beyond-the-veil experience, the subject usually loses all fear of death.

At various times in my life I have heard people say that if there is life after death why hasn't anyone ever come back to tell about it. The simple answer is that many have returned to tell about it, including Jesus Christ. Moody mentioned numerous examples in his book, and more are presented in this book. Such stories are not considered absolute scientific proof that there is life after death but constitute a growing mountain of evidence that the flame of life is not snuffed out at death—the basic premise upon which all religion is based.

The story is told about a debate between an atheist and a Mormon bishop on the subject of whether or not there is a God.

"Have you seen him?" the atheist asked.

"No," the bishop responded.

"Have you heard his voice?"

"No."

"Have you touched him?"

"No."

"Don't tell me you've smelled him."

"No."

"Then you've tasted him?"

"No."

"If you haven't seen him, heard his voice, touched him, smelled him or tasted him, then how can you know there is a God? You can't know anything you can't experience with the five senses," the atheist concluded, thinking his logic had demolished the bishop. "Do you have any brains?" the bishop asked.

"Of course," the atheist responded, wondering what direction the bishop was taking the debate.

"Have you ever seen them?"

"No."

"Have you ever heard them?"

"No."

"Have you ever touched them?"

"No."

"Have you ever smelled or tasted them?"

"No."

"Then following your own line of reasoning," the bishop concluded, "If you can't establish the presence of a brain in your skull with any of the five senses, we must conclude you don't have one, and I certainly wouldn't want to continue a debate with a man who didn't have any brains. So if you will excuse me, sir, I'll be on my way."

Likewise, this book does not provide sensory proof that there is life after death. But it does contain substantial evidence in the form of personal experiences of individuals who slipped beyond the grave and have been allowed to return. The individuals whose stories are told in this book come from all walks of life, all ages, both the rich and the poor, some with college degrees, others who did not finish high school.

As you read the stories, imagine yourself in the role of the interviewer, sitting across the table, or next to the subject on a living room sofa. You are listening carefully while the subject relates a sacred experience, perhaps one the subject has been reluctant to tell for many years, perhaps out of fear of being laughed at. But the subject is telling it to you, maybe with some hesitation, at times filled with emotion, even to the point of shedding a few tears.

As you listen, you can feel the sincerity of the subject as he or she relates the beyond-the-veil experience. You may be a little bit skeptical at first, but out of politeness and consideration you allow the person to tell the complete story. Occasionally you ask a question.

After interviews with two or three people, you might still have some reservations about the truthfulness of what you are hearing, but after 15 or 20 interviews you have come to realize that all these people couldn't be fabricating fiction. Sure, the people were under extreme stress when they had their experiences, but there are simply too many parallels, too many common elements, too many threads of truth tying the stories together. You find yourself in agreement with the subjects, firm in the faith of a very real and tangible afterlife.

You learn from those who have seen the other side that there is no longer any reason to fear death. Increased understanding of what happens after death removes fear of death. You understand more fully that how you view death really does influence how you live life. And you become more determined to live your life in accordance with the potential pointed out to you by that God who gave you life.

Publisher's note: If, after reading these stories, you are aware of a similar account, experienced by you or a loved one, that you think would be an appropriate addition to the growing body of evidence that the human soul lives beyond the grave, we invite you to tell us about the account on cassette tape and send it to us for possible publication in a future edition of *Beyond the Veil*.

Please include appropriate addresses and phone numbers in the event we wish to obtain permission to publish the story.

Send possible contributions for future editions of *Beyond the Veil* to:

Beyond the Veil
Cedar Fort Incorporated
1182 N. Industrial Park Dr.
Orem, Utah 84057

Chapter One

Everything Was Green
by Larry Tooley

We felt we had the world at our feet that Indian summer of 1972. My wife, Georgia, and I had just moved into our first house, a charming two-bedroom rambler. Three weeks prior we had been blessed with a beautiful set of twins—a bald-headed, blue-eyed boy and a sweet, petite girl. Our family was perfectly rounded out with our two older children, Larry, age six, and Lori, age three. After all, here I was thirty years old, I had a good job with a progressive electrical company, a perfect family, a new home, and the whole world before me.

I had been working on a warehouse in North Salt Lake for several weeks and was about to finish the job. We were converting it into a small factory. The majority of the work had to be done from a rolling scaffold because the ceiling was thirty feet high. We had finished installing all of the necessary lighting and outlets. All that remained was to hook up a thirty-horsepower compressor. It was located in the far corner of the building opposite the electrical panel. Because of the distance involved, it was necessary to install a junction box at the midway point. Things had gone smoothly up to this point.

On the eighteenth of September we had just signed the papers on our new house. That night Georgia and I had been talking about the job. It was then that she learned I had been working on a scaffold all this time. She objected loud and clear. She said this was the reason for an unmistakable feeling she had of impending disaster. She begged and pleaded with me not to go to work the next day. She asked me to call in sick, to do anything but go to work. I just put her off by telling her there wasn't anyone but me to finish the job and that it had to be finished the next day.

The following morning she verbally attacked me again. When she found she couldn't change my mind, she finally relented, but not without a last warning for me to be careful.

The work proceeded as expected. The wire had been pulled into the junction box from the compressor by midmorning. Because of the company's work schedule we could only shut the power off during their lunch hour. My helper and I went to lunch early and returned about 11:30. We then got into position to push the heavily insulated wires through the conduit—he on the scaffold, I at the panel.

The wire stopped when it reached the conduit's ninety-degree bend. Our repeated efforts to push it through were in vain. Out of final frustration, I climbed the scaffold from the other end. I hadn't trusted the scaffold from the very beginning. If anyone either came up or down while I was on top, I would always kneel in the corner to help assure better balance. I watched as my helper climbed down the other side and began walking away.

Then it happened. The scaffold tottered and fell as if pushed by a giant hand. Eyewitnesses to the accident later said that as the scaffold began to fall, I jumped up and grabbed the crossmembers or ceiling joists to keep from falling. As the scaffold continued on over, the lifeline hooked me behind the knees, pulling me loose and flinging me to the floor like a sling shot.

I landed feet first, fracturing both feet and driving the bones of the legs together, resulting in compound fractures. The left knee was shattered. As I was wrenched free from the cross-members, my right shoulder was pulled from the socket, and the ligaments that give the arm lifting power were ripped loose. After hitting the floor, I fell onto my right shoulder, permanently damaging the rotator cup. I then pitched forward peeling my scalp back and crushing my frontal cavities. The shock of the fall killed me.

A plumber who had been working in the warehouse at the time heard me scream as I narrowly missed him on the way down. Other workers came running, but as they saw me lying there with all the broken bones and blood, they made for the nearest exit. The sight of my broken body made them sick. Only the plumber had the presence of mind to do anything. He jumped in and pulled me out of the twisted scaffolding and proceeded to give me mouth-to-mouth resuscitation and closed heart massage.

After I hit the floor, I lay there for a brief moment and looked about. I remember feeling no pain. I noticed that everything had a green tint or hue to it. My spirit began to rise off the floor towards the ceiling. The closer I came to the ceiling, the more dense the green mist became. Eventually I found myself engulfed in a green fog.

I stopped and looked about. In every direction there seemed to be floating an endless sea of agonized souls. I experienced the uttermost feelings of despair. I thought I was in hell. The feeling of utter frustration was unbearable. I wanted so badly to get away from these tortured souls that I almost screamed from the agony I felt.

Then I was in a room looking back at an arched doorway beyond which swirled the green fog so thick it was almost black. I knew I never wanted to go back through it again. Two men had just left me and were proceeding down a hallway to my right. They had helped me put on a garment I was supposed to wear. It was a loose-fitting white robe which hung midway past my knees.

Just to the right of the arched door was seated an old man at a desk. He was writing something in a large book, as if keeping tally on the number of garments that went out each day, almost like a record keeper.

Behind me and to my left stood a man waiting for me to finish my robe adjustments. I recognized him as Larry, a friend that I had grown up with who had died in 1966, just six years earlier. He said he was to be my guide until I became oriented.

The room seemed to be made of crystallized marble of a soft pink hue. Another door, opposite the one I had entered, opened onto a street. Several low benches of white crystallized marble were against the wall. The doorways in the room had no doors, and the window openings had no panes.

As Larry and I left and entered the street, I was acutely aware of everything around me. I've never felt more fully alive. All my senses were increased a hundred-fold. I possessed superior knowledge and intelligence, qualities I knew I had always possessed, but had somehow been restricted or suppressed while I was in the physical world.

I felt like I had returned home. I knew where I was and where I was to go. We had only traveled a short distance down the street, when I stopped beside a building that I recognized. I had frequented it on many occasions. I told Larry I had to go inside before we could go any further.

Inside, a group of men were having a meeting. I felt it was important that I talk to them. I spoke in earnest, imploring them to reconsider my premature entry into the spirit world. I knew somehow that I had died prematurely and had not finished my work upon the earth. Emphatically, I drove my point home by pounding with my fist on the corner of a desk.

After my presentation, I again joined Larry outside. We continued our journey. We came upon a large, beautiful park. A large group of people were happily awaiting us. As we came up to them, the closest member of the group approached me—a beautiful young woman dressed in the whitest, most brilliant robe of the finest material I've ever seen. Her complexion was white and creamy, her hair jet black in color. She was overjoyed to see me and threw her arms around me, embracing me fondly.

She said she was my sister who had died when she was just three days old. Everyone else in the group was a relative who had died. They were all extremely happy that I was there. We talked, it seemed, for hours. They thought I might be granted a second chance to go back. They impressed upon me how deeply their wants and needs were tied to the things that only I or their living relatives could do.

When our meeting was over, and they had all departed, Larry informed me that I was being summoned to a council meeting being held in my behalf. When we arrived I was escorted into a beautiful pavilion. It consisted of two semicircles with three-tiered stadium bleachers facing each other. These too were made of brilliantly white, crystallized marble.

In the center was a six-foot square marble platform where three people stood, their backs to me. All around the ground was soft and fleecy like the top of a cloud. It appeared we were standing on clouds.

I stopped ten feet inside the entrance to the stadium. I looked about me at the men seated in the bleachers. They were in groups of two's and three's talking among themselves. I knew they were considering my request.

Only a short time had passed when they all stopped what they were doing and looked smilingly at the three men on the platform. The trio turned to face me.

The one on the right was the same height as me. He had a full head of curly hair and a short, curly beard. The man in the middle was a good half a head taller than the other two and sported a full head of curly hair and a curly beard. His hair was streaked with gray. His robe was opened halfway down his chest. All three men were barefooted.

I thought as I looked at them that they must be Peter, James and John. The one in the middle, the tallest of the three, came over and stood by my side. As he turned, he put his right arm around my shoulders. He towered above me as he looked into my eyes. He grinned the biggest, broadest grin, revealing two rows of pearly white teeth. He squeezed my shoulder affectionately. I knew that my request had been granted.

I awoke in the hospital. The days that followed were a blur of drugged sleep and relentless operations as they began to reconstruct my broken body. Deftly, my doctor performed a miracle. At first, he informed my worried wife that he didn't expect me to live past the week. If by chance I did, I would never walk again.

What he didn't know was that I was promised that I would regain my health and again lead an active and useful life. I would be able to raise my family, although my life was not to be without pain and hardship.

I eventually acquired my journeyman's electrician license and got back into construction. My physical health is fully restored. There have been times when I felt bitterness and resentment for all the pain and heartache I have had to go through.

Georgia has been my greatest help through all this. It has not been easy for her. She has suffered a mild heart seizure and undergone a nervous breakdown. We have gone through therapy to bring our lives into a normal balance. I now hold a job with a national steel company which has given us unbelievable security. I know the rest of my life has got to be good, for I've gone through enough hell already.

I am where I was before the accident, starting back up, my whole future ahead of me, thanks to a second chance granted by those three men from beyond the veil.

Chapter Two

Danny's Mission
by Vicki Kimball Wilkins

While growing up I had a special boy cousin named Danny. We were the same age and good friends. Our families lived just a few blocks away from each other, in Utah. Danny was the second in a family of six children. I was the oldest in a family of five children.

Our families went on picnics and camping trips together and always spent Christmas together at Grandma's house. Danny and I attended the same school and had the same fourth- and sixth-grade teachers. Danny kept our schoolroom busy with snakes, lizards, spiders and bugs. He loved animals and enjoyed catching them in the fields near his home.

Danny always watched out for me. Even during sixth-grade dances, he would make sure that I was not left out by asking me to dance.

During that sixth-grade year, we would often babysit together on weekends for our Aunt Peggy. She had a new baby girl. We liked babysitting together because Aunt Peggy would let us make cookies, or she would have special goodies for us to eat. Danny and I enjoyed each other's company and usually giggled a lot. Danny loved to tell jokes and tease.

We were excited in anticipation of summer at the end of our sixth-grade year. Our families planned a big camping trip up Butterfield Canyon. We were excited about all the usual things. We loved riding our mini-bikes, playing games, and roasting marshmallows around the campfire.

When we arrived in the canyon, we were as excited and happy as children can be. In addition to the fun and games, we enjoyed the camp with its scenic mountains, stream, and trees. We were having a great time until the accident.

We were riding the mini-bikes around camp and were wearing our helmets as our parents required. Danny and my brother and a friend rode the bikes up the road to check out an old mining site. On the way back to camp, Danny was in front.

Back at camp, I remember seeing a car speeding up the dirt road leaving a trail of dust. I remember our parents yelling at the car to slow down as it raced past our camp.

As the car rounded the corner above camp, it was going too fast to stop and swerved into Danny who was coming from the other direction. My brother, who was just behind Danny, saw the cloud of dust and Danny lying in the road. My brother raced to camp, yelling for someone to come and help. He said Danny was hurt real bad.

I ran as fast as I could up the road where I saw Danny lying face up in the dirt. He was very still. I was horrified. All I could do was yell for someone to hurry. Within seconds, our families were there helping to give him mouth-to-mouth resuscitation.

Carefully, they lifted him on blankets in the back of Grandpa's truck and left for the hospital. My aunt, uncle, grandpa, grandma, and mother went with him. As they drove away, they were still giving him mouth-to-mouth resuscitation.

All of us were devastated. I went into our camper and cried. I knelt down and asked my Heavenly Father to let Danny live. I know that everyone else in camp was praying too, at least in their hearts.

It seemed hours before my aunt and uncle and mother came back. My mother hugged me and told me that Danny had died. I couldn't believe it. It couldn't be true.

I saw my uncle tell his children. Everyone was crying. No one could believe it.

I walked over to my aunt's camper. I told her I was so sorry. She hugged me for a long time. She was sobbing. I was numb.

We packed up to leave. On the way home, I asked my mother what had happened at the hospital. She said the doctors worked on Danny a long time, then called my aunt and uncle into a private room and told them that Danny had died.

A few days later we went to Danny's funeral. He was in a beautiful light blue casket. He looked so different to me. I was used to seeing him grinning and so full of life.

The speaker spoke of Danny's love for life and love for nature and animals. He talked about Danny's love for Scouting and Primary. Then a lady sang "Oh Danny Boy." It was a sad funeral, and everything seemed so unreal to me. We took Danny out to the cemetery and buried him next to Grandpa.

As the days and years went by, I really missed Danny. I could feel my aunt watching me and thinking that Danny and I would have been involved in a lot of the same things since we were the same age in school. I knew it was hard for her.

A few years later, my uncle was transferred to California. They moved into a beautiful home with a swimming pool. They were not active in church.

During my senior year, we drove to California to spend Christmas at Disneyland. We spent a day with my aunt and uncle. It was good to see them again. Everyone was growing up. But there was a real void without Danny. Seeing the family again brought back many painful memories.

After graduation, I attended Weber State College. I lived in an apartment close to campus with five other girls. It was my first time away from home. During the middle of the school year, I had a dream. It was so real I can still remember every detail. It is as clear to me today as the night it happened.

In the dream I was at my parents' home. I heard a knock at the door. I opened it. I was totally surprised. Danny was standing there. I recognized him even though he was a young man. He looked 19 or 20. He was grinning, just like he used to. He stood about 5'9" and had a strong build like his father. His hair was short in a missionary-style cut and was parted on the right side and combed back. His hair was a sandy blond, a little darker than I remembered it.

He wore a navy blue suit with a tie of the same color. His shirt was white and on the lapel of the suit he wore one of those white missionary badges that said, "Elder Daniel Chapman."

"What are you doing?" I asked.

"I'm a missionary," he answered, still smiling. "I need you to come with me."

"OK," I said.

All of a sudden we were walking down an unfamiliar stairway into a large family room. Danny's family was there. I watched as Danny went over to his father, who was reading the newspaper. Danny tried to teach him something about the gospel of Jesus Christ, but my uncle was too busy to look up.

Then Danny went over to my aunt, who was quilting. He began talking to her, to teach her, too. He was pleading with all his heart, but she didn't acknowledge his presence either. I remember wondering why they couldn't hear him. I could hear every word.

Then Danny went over to his brothers and sisters, who were sitting on the floor watching television. He tried to get their attention, but they would not take their eyes off the screen. Danny wanted them to listen to the gospel. He wanted to teach them.

Danny finally turned to me. I was still standing in the doorway, watching.

"See, Vicki," he said, his face serious. "They can't hear me. You have to teach them."

I woke up crying. The dream had been so real. I wondered why his family couldn't hear him. Danny was alive. He was in the spirit world. He was a missionary. He loved the gospel and wanted his family to hear it, to know that it was true. He wanted his family to be sealed together in the temple, for time and all eternity.

After the dream I did not contact the family immediately but prayed that I would know when the time was right. I was afraid of somehow offending them. My uncle and aunt are very good people and are very much oriented towards family values. They are members of The Church of Jesus Christ of Latter-day Saints and have had all of their children baptized. The children sometimes attended Primary and Sunday School, but my aunt and uncle always stayed home.

With time, my uncle received an opportunity to move back to Utah. He and his family returned to the same neighborhood where they had lived before, but to a different house.

That year we had our Christmas Eve family party at my uncle's new home. As I walked down the stairway into the family room I recognized it as

the same place Danny and I had gone to see them in
the dream. I could feel goose bumps all over me.

I didn't say anything to my aunt and uncle at
the time, but in the months to come I told each of
their children what had happened. They all
responded warmly to my story.

A year later I attended BYU. One day I was in
a bookstore looking for some things for school
when I was prompted to pick up a book, *A
Marvelous Work and a Wonder*, by LeGrand
Richards. I had never read the book, but when I
tried to put it back on the shelf, I felt strongly
prompted that I should buy the book for my aunt.
So I bought one for her and one for me.

I didn't give her the book right away. The
right opportunity didn't present itself. I think I was
a little afraid, and I am not sure why.

Later that same spring I was married in the
Salt Lake Temple. After the honeymoon, we
moved into a home we rented from my
grandmother. We had only been there a few days
and were unpacking boxes, when I came across the
two books that I had been prompted to buy. I told
my husband about the dream, and everything else
that had happened. He said I should tell my aunt
and uncle about the dream and give them the book.
He said the book was one of the best missionary
books ever written.

As he was telling me this, there was a knock at the door. It was my grandmother, with my aunt and uncle. I couldn't believe it. My husband gave me that look, like I'd better tell them what was going on.

As we greeted them at the door, my grandmother explained that they had come to fix the ceiling fan. After a few minutes I went into the bedroom and offered a prayer that I would know what to say to them. I was impressed that I should give the book to my aunt and just tell her about my dream.

So while my grandmother and uncle were working on the fan, I called my aunt into the bedroom. We sat on the bed and I told her everything. She cried when I told her about the dream. She said she hoped it was true and that Danny was a missionary.

I gave her the book. She hugged me and said she would read it. She said she loved to read. The Spirit was strong, and I knew that she knew in her heart that my dream was true.

When my uncle called my aunt to come into the front room, she quickly wiped away the tears and put the book in her purse. She thanked me.

Shortly after that my husband and I moved out of state to attend college. Whenever we have been back for visits and I see my aunt, she always hugs me and says she is reading the book. She always wants me to tell her about the dream again and describe how Danny looked. She says she misses him and thinks about him a lot.

I have never felt like the time was right to relate the experience to my uncle. I recently asked my aunt if she had told him. She said that she had not and wanted me to do it. I told her I would about the time I was preparing this story for publication. I told her I felt the time was finally right. I believe with all my heart that when they begin listening to the missionary lessons, Danny will be watching and helping from beyond the veil.

Chapter Three

I Wanted Those Two Little Girls
by Janet Christensen

My grandmother, Bertha Deusnup Elder, had a hard life as the wife of Jonathan Pratt Elder. They moved a lot as the family went from farm to farm establishing new homesteads. Often their living conditions were primitive—no running water, no electricity, no telephones, sometimes no neighbors within miles.

As they moved, the family continued to grow, until by 1913, while living in Alberta, Canada, Bertha had given birth to 13 children. After much deliberation, she decided that life was just too difficult for her to bring any more children into the world.

It wasn't long afterwards that Bertha became seriously ill. I don't remember the nature of the illness, only that it was sufficiently serious that a nurse whom Bertha called Sister Edwards came to the home to care for her. In those days, in remote rural communities, going to hospitals was usually out of the question.

With Sister Edwards sitting beside her bed, Bertha suddenly realized she was rising in the air above her bed, the pain and discomfort of a few moments earlier was suddenly gone. As she looked down at her bed, she could see Sister Edwards sitting beside the bed.

Thinking Bertha had died, Sister Edwards later said she wanted to call to the others in the house, but was prompted to do nothing. She had a peaceful feeling that everything would be all right if she just waited a few minutes.

Bertha felt relieved. The pain was gone. She was so full of peace, that she had no particular desire to return to her body.

She was greeted by a woman who escorted her into a large room where she was greeted by many of her departed friends. One was a young man she had befriended and encouraged to develop his artistic talents. He was sitting in front of an easel, painting. Though he was very happy to see Bertha, he quickly returned to his work as though his time was very precious.

Bertha was then taken into another room where there were many children. On the far side of the room she saw two little girls, whom she did not know. They were so beautiful she could not look away from them.

"Do you want them?" the guide asked.

"Yes. Oh, yes," she responded quickly. "Can I return to earth life and have them?"

"Yes," said the escort. "That is the purpose of this visit, to let you see them. Now we must return." Bertha returned to her body, much to the relief of Sister Edwards. After recovering from the illness, Bertha told Jonathan she wanted more children.

A year later, after moving to Oakley, Idaho, Bertha gave birth to a new little girl whom she named Alberta. Two years later she delivered another little girl, LaVirle. For the remainder of her life, Bertha insisted these were the two little girls she had seen in the large room.

Shortly after the birth of the second little girl the family moved back to Raymond, Alberta, Canada to establish a new homestead. In a severe flu epidemic in 1919, Bertha became critically ill again. Alberta was four years old. Bertha passed away again, but this time she did not come back. Family members wondered why she was not allowed to raise those two little girls, considering the special circumstances surrounding their births.

It wasn't until years later, when Alberta received a patriarchal blessing that a reason was given. She was told in the blessing that her mother had been able to raise her more effectively from beyond the veil. Both women were spiritual in nature, often acting upon promptings of the spirit.

After Bertha's death, Alberta could not be comforted. She was only four and a half years old but could not understand why her mother was gone. No one could comfort her.

Suddenly one day, everyone noticed the little girl was happy. When they asked her what had happened, she described her mother appearing to her. She described wanting to throw her arms around her mother, but Bertha wouldn't let her. The family surmised the reason for this was that Bertha had become a spirit without a body. The spirit of the mother comforted the little girl, telling her that everything would be fine.

In 1972, when her youngest daughter Lori was 12, Alberta was driving with her daughter Dana and her husband Raeldon Barker from Alberta to Portland. They were driving through a mountain pass near Sandpoint, Idaho, when on slippery roads they crashed head-on into a truck.

Dana and Raeldon suffered no more than a few bruises and cuts, but Alberta was not breathing. Dana began giving her mouth-to-mouth resuscitation while a passing motorist helped them bring her to the hospital in Sandpoint. Raeldon called the local Mormon bishop and asked for assistance in giving her a blessing.

The first thing Alberta remembered after the wreck was how good she felt. The pain was gone. The asthma no longer bothered her. She felt wonderful.

She found herself in a large room surrounded by many people whom she had known, who had died. She was so happy to be free from pain and visiting with loved ones.

Then her attention was focused back in the operating room. With the doctors looking on, Raeldon and the bishop were blessing her. She could hear Raeldon saying she still had responsibilities on earth.

Alberta realized she had a choice. She could stay and be part of this wonderful new place, or she could return and be burdened again with poor health and family problems. She wanted to stay in the new place, but when she heard Raeldon say she still had responsibilities on earth, she thought of her two youngest daughters and decided to return.

The next thing she knew she was on the operating table. She remembered going into the large room, visiting with those people, and making the decision to return. But she couldn't remember the names and faces of the people she had seen. She knew only that she had recognized them at the time.

Four years later, Alberta passed away, this time to remain on the other side of the veil.

Chapter Four

Tremendous Mental Agility

In October, 1987, I was headed north on I-15 towards Salt Lake City when I saw an elderly man, who had become disoriented, driving south in the north-bound lane, headed straight for me. I don't remember what happened, but from what others told me afterwards, I apparently tried to avoid the elderly man because when he hit me I spun around and was hit head-on again by another north-bound car.

The old man died within three or four minutes. Those who stopped to help said I was not breathing, nor could they detect any heartbeat. I was so badly crushed inside the car that it took three ambulance crews an hour and a half to get me out. The dashboard was smashed against my chest. My face and eyes were seriously injured. My thigh bone was pushed up through the hip socket. The socket alone was broken in seventeen places, and there were eight other breaks in my hip.

From the time of the accident until I was well along the road to recovery, I lost track of time. When I regained consciousness, I began to remember some strange events that were recorded clearly in my memory. I remember being in a beautiful white, light-filled cloud. It might have been just a mist or bright fog. I knew there were things beyond the fog that I wasn't supposed to see. There was an enormous feeling of peace, everywhere. The peace was associated with a complete awareness of the presence of God and his influence. His presence was there, though I could not see him, nor could I see anyone else.

I had a tremendous mental agility. My mind was so quick, and I was able to see in every direction at the same time. I realized later I was not seeing with my natural eyes. I was perceiving and comprehending everything around me. At the same time, I was feeling an enormous mental capacity. It was nothing new. I was aware that I had always been this way. It felt very natural. It was the real me. I didn't have to think about it. That was the natural way of things, and I felt very comfortable, very relaxed.

At the same time, I had the distinct feeling that there was something on the other side of the cloud that I was not being permitted to see, but I knew in my heart that if I were permitted to see it, I would be able to comprehend everything immediately.

The mental agility I experienced, the ability to comprehend, was different than what we know in this life. If you were going to teach me about tape recorders, for example, you would use clumsy, cumbersome words. You would tell me how tape recorders are made, the electronic components used, and the function of each. Then you would show me the mechanics of how to open the cassette and put in the tapes, how to close the door then push the various buttons, and the functions of each. You would show me how to control the volume, attach a remote mike, and how to operate it on batteries or by plugging it into an outlet. Little by little I would become proficient in the use of a tape recorder.

But in the mental state I was experiencing in that cloud, none of your instructions would be necessary. All you would have to do is show me the tape recorder and I would be able to comprehend everything about it, instantly, even if I had never seen one before. My ability to comprehend and learn had been multiplied a thousand times or more. The slow, clunky manner in which I learned on earth had evaporated. I could absorb and comprehend things I never thought possible.

I have no idea what the time parameters were to this experience. I don't know if it was ten hours, ten minutes, or ten seconds. And I don't remember the transition when I left that beautiful bright cloud and returned to my body. I didn't see my body from above, nor did I see anyone doing anything with my body.

When this memory came back to me, I was in the hospital, and in so much pain I could hardly communicate with the people around me. I was cognizant when awake, but I slept a lot. There were times when I thought for sure I was going to die. I didn't know a person could hurt that much and live.

While in the hospital, when the suffering was at its peak, I was visited by a heavenly being. Without words, with a form of communication far more complete, he told me he loved me with a perfect love and that he wanted me to become one with him. I felt the pure generosity of that statement. It was a communication from soul to soul. I struggle to put it in words. Feelings accompanied the ideas as they were communicated. He also told me that as I became one with him he wanted me to help my brothers and sisters in the human family become one with him too, because he loved them the same as he loved me.

There was one particular day in the hospital when I could feel the prayers that people were offering for me. What I felt was powerful. The prayers were in my room, in the air, all around me. I felt like I could reach out my hand and touch them. It seemed they were almost tangible. In sensing the prayers, I also felt the love of the people who had offered them.

I am convinced that it was by the mercy of God that I was allowed to experience the prayers people were offering for me. I just hope they realize their prayers were meaningful and made a difference. Since that time, when I pray for someone, I do so with increased faith, knowing my prayers have power.

Feeling the love of my Father in Heaven and the prayers of my family and friends gave me the strength I needed to face the pain and a very difficult recovery. The love I felt through these experiences meant more to me than the experience of being dead and coming back.

When I was dead, I was just me. I was not any happier or sadder. Everything about me was me. That was all.

Before the accident I was a very competitive person, always wanting the highest grade, the best job, the most money. I think I'm different now. I think I love and appreciate other people more and have a stronger desire to do things for others.

Almost every day I think about my journey beyond the veil and the experience of feeling my

Heavenly Father's love. I feel myself changing, I think for the better.

Chapter Five

As a Mother I Had Not Failed
by Rita Schetselaar

The day began normally enough. Michael and I arose at the usual hour to have breakfast and to attend the usual morning preparations. He left with his father at 7 a.m. to go to the fields.

I quickly did the breakfast dishes and lay down on the couch to grab a few precious moments of rest. Baby Alan was asleep in the bassinet in his room. He was such a good baby, sleeping four to five hours between feedings at this eight-week stage of his life.

Alan awoke at 8 a.m. and we enjoyed his breakfast feeding together. Since Alan preferred the more shallow car bed to his deep bassinet, I placed him in it and put it on my bed so that I could do the ironing in his room.

Once Alan was settled, I set about doing the ironing. I had learned to sit, rather than stand, to accomplish this task and did so at this time. Ordinarily, I enjoyed ironing, and as I began that morning, I was cheerful enough, even humming as I worked. However, before I had worked long, an incredible weariness overcame me. I thought I had adjusted fairly well to the frequent interruptions to my sleep, but on this particular morning I found myself resting my head on the ironing board and closing my eyes.

Deciding that further efforts to iron were pointless, I laid down on the extra bed in Alan's room. Sometime during the morning I heard Michael come in through the back door, go downstairs to his tool room, and leave again without coming in to see me or his son. A little later I heard Alan cry out, but his cries were brief, so I thought he had gone back to sleep and didn't go to check.

I awoke with a start about 11 a.m. when Aunt Rea stopped by. She started down the hall to the room where Alan was sleeping, but she turned back when I asked her not to disturb him.

When Aunt Rea was gone, I hurried to prepare Michael's lunch. I finished by noon, and since Michael hadn't come home yet, I decided to take Alan with me to take lunch to his father in the fields.

As I started down the short hall towards my bedroom, I felt a chill. I shrugged it off and continued towards the door. It bothered me that I couldn't remember closing the door.

Cautiously, I opened the door. I could see Alan in the corner of the car bed. He wasn't moving. The chill returned. He looked too still, like he wasn't breathing.

"He can't be. . . ," I thought as I rushed to him. But he was. He was dead. He had suffocated with his face into the vinyl bumper pad that lined the inside of the car bed.

During the weeks to come I struggled with the knowledge that I might have prevented Alan's death. It became increasingly difficult to go to sleep on the bed where Alan had died while I slept.

During the third week following Alan's death, I was lying in bed wide awake one night. Michael was asleep beside me, but I could not even close my eyes.

Suddenly I looked up to see Alan standing in the hall just beyond the open doorway to our room. I remember being surprised that I recognized him because he was adult in stature. He was tall, taller than his 6'2" father. He did not speak, and yet I heard within my soul the answers to the questions that had tormented me during the weeks since his death.

Suddenly I knew that Alan's death was not untimely. He was where he was supposed to be. I knew that I was not responsible for his death. My extreme weariness had been a necessary condition to overcome my natural instincts to answer every one of his slight cries with an on-the-spot, visual check. I knew that I had not failed as a mother, and I would not be punished any further.

Alan stood there for a few moments only, allowing me to absorb the peace that he brought, both through his presence and the messages that filled my mind and heart. As I lay there wondering whether or not to wake his father or speak to him aloud, he smiled once more and left. Alan's visit from beyond the veil brought the first restful, peaceful sleep I had known in weeks.

Chapter Six

Everyone Had Something to Do
by Heber Q. Hale

It is with a very humble and grateful spirit that I attempt to relate on this occasion by request, a personal experience which is very sacred to me. I must of necessity be brief. Furthermore there were certain things made known to me which I do not feel at liberty to relate here. Let me say by way of preface that between the hours of twelve and seven-thirty on the night of January 20, 1920, while alone in a room at the home of my friend W.J. Brawson in Carey, Idaho, this glorious manifestation was given to me.

I was not conscious of anything that transpired during the hours mentioned except what I experienced in this manifestation. I did not turn over in bed nor was I disturbed by any sound, which is unusual for me. Whether it be called a dream, an apparition, a vision or a pilgrimage of my spirit into the world of spirits I care not. I know I actually saw and experienced the things related in this heavenly manifestation, and they are as real to me as any experience in my life. For me, at least, this is sufficient.

Of all the doctrines and practices of the Church, the vicarious work for the dead has been the most difficult for me to comprehend and whole-heartedly accept. I consider this vision the Lord's answer to the prayer of my soul on this and certain other questions.

I passed but a short distance from my body through a film in the world of spirits. This was my first experience after going to sleep. I seemed to realize I had passed through the change called death. I mentioned this in my first conversation with the immortal beings with whom I immediately came in contact.

I readily observed their displeasure of the use of the word "death" and the fear which we attach to it. There, they use another word in referring to the transition from mortality, which word I do not now recall. I can only approach its meaning as the impression was left upon my mind, by calling it the new birth.

My first visual impression was the nearness of the world of spirits to the world of mortality. The vastness of this heavenly sphere was bewildering to the eyes of my spirit. Many of those I saw enjoyed unrestricted freedom of both vision and action. The vegetation and landscape was beautiful beyond description, like the rainbow, not all green, but gold with various shades of pink, orange, and lavender. A sweet calmness pervaded everything. The people I met there I did not think of as spirits, but as men and women—self-thinking, self-acting individuals going about important business in a most orderly manner. There was perfect order, and everyone had something to do and seemed to be about their business.

I learned the inhabitants of the spirit world are classified according to how they lived and their obedience to the Father's will. Particularly, I observed that the wicked and unrepentant are confined to a certain district by themselves, the confines of which are definitely determined and impassible as the line marking the division of the physical and spiritual world, a mere film but impassible until the person himself has changed. The world of spirits is the temporary abode of all spirits, pending the resurrection from the dead and the judgment.

There was much activity within the different spheres, and I saw appointed ministers coming from the higher to the lower places in pursuit of their missionary appointments.

I had a very pronounced desire to meet certain of my kinfolk and friends, but I was at once impressed with the fact that I had entered a tremendously great and extensive world, even greater than our earth and more numerously inhabited. I could be in only one place at a time, could look in only one direction at a time, and accordingly it would require many years to search out and converse with all those I had known and those whom I desired to meet, unless they were especially summoned to receive me.

All worthy men and women were appointed to special and regular work. There was a well-organized plan of action. It was directed principally towards preaching the gospel to the unconverted, teaching those who sought knowledge, establishing family relationships, and gathering genealogies for the use and benefit of mortal relatives who were vicariously performing baptisms and sealing ordinances for the departed in the temples on earth.

The authorized representatives of families in the world of spirits have access to our temple records and are kept fully advised of the work therein. But the vicarious work done by mortals does not become automatically effective unless the recipients first repent and accept baptism and confirmation. Then certain consummating ordinances are performed in the spirit world.

So the great work is going on with them doing a work there which we cannot do here, and we doing a work here which they cannot do—both parts necessary, each the complement of the other. Thus, spirits and mortals are bringing about the salvation of all God's children who will be saved.

I was surprised to find there no babies in arms. I met the infant son of Arson W. Rawlings, my first counselor, and immediately recognized him as the baby who died a few years earlier. Yet he seemed to have the intelligence and, in certain respects, the appearance of an adult. He was engaged in matters pertaining to his family and its genealogy.

My mind was quite content on the point that mothers will again receive into their arms their children who die in infancy and will be fully satisfied. The entrance into the world of spirits is not an inhibition of growth but a great opportunity for development. Earthly babies are adult spirits in infant bodies.

I beheld a mighty multitude of men, the largest I have ever seen gathered in one place, whom I immediately recognized as soldiers. They were the millions who had been savagely slaughtered and rushed into the world of spirits during World War I.

. . .

As I passed on, I met my beloved mother. She greeted me most affectionately and expressed surprise at seeing me there and reminded me that I had not completed my allotted mission on earth. She seemed to be going somewhere and was in a hurry and accordingly took leave, saying she would see me again.

I moved forward, covering an appreciable distance and consuming considerable time viewing the wonderful landscapes, parks, trees, and flowers, and meeting people, some of whom I knew but many thousands whom I did not recognize.

I presently approached a small group of men standing in a path lined with spacious stretches of flowers, grasses, and shrubbery, all of a golden hue, marking the approach to a beautiful building. The men were engaged in earnest conversation. One of their number parted from the rest and came walking down the path. I at once recognized former Church President Joseph F. Smith whom I had known in the flesh. He embraced me as a father would a son and, after a few words of greeting, quickly remarked, "You have not come to stay."

For the first time, I became fully aware of my incomplete mission on earth and, as much as I would have liked to remain, I at once asked President Smith if I might return.

"You have expressed a righteous desire," he replied, "And I shall take the matter up with the authorities and let you know later." He then turned and led me toward the little group of men from whom he had just separated. I immediately recognized Brigham Young and the Prophet Joseph Smith and was surprised to find the former of shorter and heavier build than I expected to find him. All three of these men were in possession of a calm and holy majesty, which was at once kind and kingly. President Smith introduced me to the others, who greeted me warmly. We then returned to our original place. President Smith took his leave, saying he would see me again.

From a certain point of vantage, I was permitted to view this earth and what was going on here. There were no limitations to my vision and I was astonished at this. I saw my wife and children at home. I saw President Heber J. Grant at the head of the great Church and kingdom of God, and felt the divine power that radiated from God giving the Church light and truth, guiding its destiny.

I beheld this nation founded as it is upon correct principles and designed to endure and beset by evil and sinister forces that seek to lead men astray and thwart the purposes of God. I saw towns and cities, the sin and wickedness of men and women. I saw vessels sailing upon the ocean and scanned the battle-scarred fields of France and Belgium. I saw the whole world as if it were a panorama passing before my eyes.

Then there came to me the unmistakable impression that this earth and persons upon it are open to the visions of the spirit only when special permission is given or when they are assigned to special service. This is particularly true of the righteous who are busily engaged in the service of the Lord and cannot be engaged in two fields of activity at the same time.

The wicked and unrepentant spirits, still having their free agency and applying themselves in no useful or wholesome undertaking, seek pleasure about their old haunts to the extent they are still tools of Satan. It is idle, mischievous, and deceptive spirits who appear as miserable counterfeits at spiritualistic scenes, table dancing, and other such things. The noble and great men and women do not respond at the call of the mediums and every curious group of meddlesome inquirers. They would not do it in mortality, and they certainly do not do it in their increased state of knowledge in the world of immortality. The wicked and unrepentant spirits are allies of Satan and his hosts operating through willing mediums in the flesh. These three forces constitute an unholy trinity upon the earth and all are responsible for wickedness among men and nations.

I moved forward, feasting my eyes upon the beauty. Everything about me was glowing in indescribable peace and happiness which abounded in everybody and through everything. The further I went the more glorious things appeared.

While standing at a certain vantage point I beheld a short distance away a wonderfully beautiful temple. It was capped with golden domes. Coming from the temple was a small group of men dressed in robes, who paused for a brief conversation. These were the first I had seen thus clad. The millions I had previously seen were dressed, of course, but dressed variously, the soldiers, for instance, were in uniforms.

In this little group of holy men, my eyes rested upon one more splendid and holy than all the rest. President Smith parted from the others and came to my side.

"Do you know him?" he asked. I quickly answered that I did. My eyes beheld the Lord and Savior. My soul was filled with rapture and unspeakable joy.

President Smith informed me that I had been given permission to return and complete my mission upon the earth, which the Lord had appointed me to fill.

"Brother Heber, you have a great work to do," he said, his hand on my shoulder. "Go forward with all your heart, and you shall be blessed in your mission. From this time on, never doubt that God lives, that Jesus Christ is his son, the redeemer of the world, and that the Holy Ghost is a God of spirit and the messenger for the Father and the Son. Never doubt the resurrection of the dead and the immortality of the soul. . . ." Having completed these remarks he bade me farewell.

I traveled a considerable distance through various scenes and past innumerable people before I reached the sphere where I had first entered the world of spirits. I was greeted by many friends and relatives, certain of whom sent words of greeting and council to dear ones on earth. My brother was one of them.

One other I will mention. I met Brother John Adamson, his wife, son James and daughter Isabelle, all of whom were killed by the hand of an assassin at Carey, Idaho, on the evening of October 29, 1915. They seemed to divine that I was on my way back to mortality and immediately asked me to tell their children that they were very happy, and not to mourn their departure or worry their minds over the manner by which they were taken.

"There is a purpose in it, and we have work here to do which requires our collective efforts and which we could not do individually," said Brother Adamson.

I was made to know that the work referred to was that of genealogy in which they were working in England and Scotland. One of the most sacred and great things in heaven is family relationships, the establishment of a complete chain without a broken link. The unholy and bad will be dropped out and other new links put in, or two adjoining links welded together. Men and women throughout the world are moved upon by their dead ancestors to gather genealogy. The links in the chains are the ordinances of baptism, endowments, and sealings. These ordinances, performed in the temples by the living for the dead, are the welding of the links. . . .

As I was approaching the place where I had entered, my attention was attracted to a small group of women preparing what appeared to be wearing apparel. Observing my inquiring countenance, one of the women said they were preparing to receive a friend of mine, Brother Phillip Worthington. He died two days after my experience in the spirit world. I spoke at his funeral.

As I gasped his name, I was told that if I knew the joy and glorious mission that awaited him, I would not want to ask that he be detained longer on earth.

Then flooding through my consciousness came the truth that the will of the Lord can be done on earth as it is in heaven, only when we resign completely to his will and let his will be done in innocence and peace. . . .

Men and women and children are often called to missions of great importance on the other side and some respond gladly while others refuse to go or their loved ones will not give them up. Also, many die because they have not faith to be healed. Yet others live long and pass out of this world of mortality without any special manifestations or actions of the divine will.

When a man (or woman or child) is stricken ill, the prime importance is not if he is going to live or die. What matters whether he lives or dies so long as the Father's will be done? Surely we can trust him with God. Herein lies the special duty and privilege of administration by the priesthood. It is given the elders to divine the will of the Father concerning the one upon whose head their hands are laid. If for any reason they are unable to receive the Father's will, then they shall continue to pray in faith for the afflicted and humbly concede supremacy to the will of God, that his will be done on earth as it is in heaven. . . .

Birth into the world of spirits is a glorious privilege and blessing. The greatest spirits in the family of the Father have not usually been permitted to tarry longer in the flesh than is necessary to perform a certain mission. They are called to the world of spirits where the field is greater and the workers fewer. . . .

Immediately my body was quickened, and I arose to ponder over and now declare to the world, that irrespective of what others may say or think, I do know of my own positive knowledge and from my own personal experience that Jesus Christ is the son of the Father and Savior of the world.

The spirit of man does not die but survives the change called death and goes to the world of spirits which is upon or near this world. Man's individuality is not lost in death nor his progress inhibited. The spirits will literally take up their bodies again in the Resurrection. The principles of salvation are now being taught to the spirits and the great work of saving the Father's family among the living and the dead is in progress. Comparatively few will be lost. The gospel of Jesus Christ has again been established upon the earth with all the keys, powers, authority, and blessings through the instrumentality of the prophet Joseph Smith. This is not only the power that will save and exalt everyone who is obedient, but will ultimately save the world. The burden of our mission is to save souls for God. The work for the living is no more important than the work for the dead who have passed beyond the veil.

Chapter Seven

The Most Beautiful Music I Have Ever Heard
by Elizabeth Whitehead

I remember thinking the doctors would give up on me if I didn't give them a sign. I had been gone from my body, but now I was back. I had to let them know. If I could just open an eye or wiggle a finger they would know I was there. I was in the intensive care unit at Orem Community Hospital. It was November, 1986. I had just suffered a cardiac arrest.

Because of what had just happened I no longer just believed in an afterlife. I knew for a surety there was life beyond death because I had just been there.

I was in a tunnel. The only reason I call it a tunnel is because I can't think of a better word. It was like a long valley with rounded sides.

I wasn't shown, or I can't remember the first part of the tunnel. But the part I remember is clear, like I was there yesterday. Maybe I wasn't allowed to remember what happened on first entering the tunnel.

At the end of the tunnel was a large room with a door at the far end. I don't know why the door was significant to me, only that it was. There were people in the room. I knew when I was within five feet of the end of the tunnel that if I entered the room I would not come back. I don't know how I knew that. I just knew there would be no coming back once I entered the room.

No one told me not to go into the room, and I didn't feel any fear about entering. I just didn't do it.

Human words are not adequate to describe the beauty of the room. There was a lot of light, a brightness that went beyond just white—kind of a many-colored iridescence. We don't have the words in our language to describe the beauty, not only of the room, but the people too.

It was a large room, and there were many people there, standing mostly to either side where the tunnel met the room. I didn't recognize or know any of the people. I just knew they were good people with warm, beautiful, smiling faces.

On my left was a chorus or a small choir, like a church choir, with about 20 people. They were singing the most beautiful music I have ever heard. They were singing "Nearer My God to Thee." I didn't want to leave the music behind. It was so peaceful, so warming.

Again, I don't know why I didn't stay. No one told me not to come in, and I felt no reservations. In fact I wanted to stay; I just didn't do it.

I don't remember any of the details of returning through the tunnel. I know there was a reason for what I was allowed to remember and what I don't remember.

I don't remember looking down at my body, or anything like that. Suddenly I was back again, thinking about my husband and two little children. I loved them and wanted to be with them. I knew how much they needed me. I wanted to stay on earth for them.

I remember thinking that if I could just open my eyes they would know I was there. I was afraid the doctors would give up on me if I didn't give them a sign. "We're losing her. She's gone again," the doctors were saying. I wanted desperately to tell them I was back, but I couldn't make a sound. When my eyes wouldn't open, I tried to move a little finger. I couldn't do that either.

Though I couldn't communicate with them, the doctors didn't give up on me. I was transferred to American Fork Hospital and remained in the intensive care unit for six days, eventually regaining consciousness and control of my body.

I felt like I was allowed to remember this experience beyond the veil, not only for me but to help other people put their fears of death at ease. As a result of what I experienced, I am no longer afraid to die, and I hope I can share this new confidence in an afterlife with others.

Following this experience, people whom I have known, upon losing someone close to them, have called, hoping I might be able to help set their minds at ease concerning the recently departed one. I tell them what I have seen and felt.

As I was having this kind of conversation with a friend one evening, it hit me that this was why I was given this experience, so I could help others.

We feel sorrow when someone we love passes on, but I think the sorrow is mostly for ourselves. We shouldn't ever feel it for them. They are going to a place so wonderful, so beautiful, so peaceful, that we should not feel bad for them. In fact, I would guess that most of them wouldn't want to come back, even if they could. I know these things are true because of my own brief visit beyond the veil.

Chapter Eight

Angels Save Wyoming Children

On the morning of May 16, 1986, self-proclaimed revolutionary David Young marched into an elementary school in Cokeville, Wyoming. Young promptly informed the media that if his demands for ransom were not met, he would blow up the 135 children in the school, plus their teachers and administrators. The adults in the school were told they would be shot if they didn't cooperate fully with Young.

As the day progressed, with negotiations at a standstill, numerous fervent prayers were offered by those in the school and by their loved ones on the outside. Later, when the incident was over, some of the children began talking about angels and heavenly voices. Some of these events are described in detail in the book, *Trial by Terror*, by Hart Wixom.

"They were standing there above us," Katie Walker told her parents, matter-of-factly, after it was all over. "There was a mother and a father and a lady holding a tiny baby and a little girl with long hair. There was a family of people. The woman told us the bomb was going off soon and to listen to our brother. He was going to come over and tell us what to do."

"She said to be sure we did what he told us," added Rachel, Katie's younger sister.

"They were all dressed in white, bright like a light bulb but brighter around the face," Katie told her mother.

"The girl had a long dress," Rachel added, "which covered her feet, and she had light brown hair."

"The woman made me feel good," Katie said. "I knew she loved me."

Katie said the visitors were standing in the air, about two feet above the ground. When asked how they entered the room both girls said they came down through the ceiling. All were dressed in white, but the girl's dress was longest in that it covered her feet. Katie said the lady doing the talking had brown curly hair like her mother's. When asked if the angels had wings, both girls replied they did not. "They looked like we do, but all dressed in white," Rachel emphasized.

"I didn't see anything, nothing!" the older brother, Travis, said when he was asked about the incident. "I just heard a voice. It told me to find my little sisters and take them over by the window and keep them there. I did what I was told. I looked around and found them and told them to follow me over by the window."

"I told them to stay there and not move," Travis continued. "They were playing with their friends, and I didn't think they would want to leave them. I knew they had to come with me. They got their coloring pages, and I took them over by the windows."

"I didn't stay there with them," Travis explained. "I was also told (by the voice) to help them through the window when the bomb went off. I went back over with the other boys where I had been, by the door. . . ."

When asked if he offered a prayer, Travis said he did. "I said, 'Heavenly Father, we need your help. We can't get out of this without you. Please help us know what to do.' "

Several other parents claimed their children said someone appeared to them in the hostage room. Some didn't want to talk about what happened, but some did.

Six-year-old Nathan Hartley was sitting near the taped line in the hostage room before the bomb detonated.

"A lady told me the bomb was going to go off very soon," he told his father, a veteran sheriff's department investigator. "She told me how to save myself. She said to go over by the window, then hurry out when I heard the bomb explode. She told me that I would make it if I did exactly what she said." Nathan said he had never seen the woman before.

The bomb went off, as David Young had planned, and as the angels had predicted. Though many were injured, David Young was the only one killed. Miraculously the children were saved. "Everyone involved in the investigation of David Young's bomb knows something strange and unexplainable happened," said Eva Clark, one of the adult hostages. "No one has any plausible idea at all how the children safely escaped. I think it is time to listen to them. . . and let them tell us the reason they all survived. . . ."

"I'll tell you what happened," said Rocky Moore, the local football coach and former atheist. "God was looking out for his kids."

It was about six months after the bombing when the Walker girls were looking through some photos of family members that Katie picked up an old locket with a picture in it. After carefully considering the photo, she said, "She looked like this, only she wasn't wearing glasses." She was referring to the female angel that had talked to them during the crisis. A few moments later Rachel entered the room.

"That's the angel," she declared, after examining the locket. "But without the glasses." The locket contained a photo of Shirley Ruth Thornock, the girls' grandmother, who had died when their mother was only 16 years old.

Nathan Hartley had a similar experience as he and his father were leafing through a family album. "That's her," the youngster cried, stopping his father on a page that contained a photo of the child's great-grandmother, Flossie Elliott. She had been dead for three years.

When David Young entered the Cokeville school on that spring morning in 1986, he was determined to kill a lot of children if his demands were not met. Though his bomb went off, he did not succeed in killing anyone but himself, thanks to the aid of those messengers from beyond the veil.

Trial By Terror is available at all LDS bookstores or by contacting the publisher at: Horizon Publishers, P.O. 490 Bountiful, Utah 84010-0490 (Wixom, Hart, *Trial By Terror*. Bountiful, Utah: Horizon Publishers, 1987.)

Chapter Nine

I Was Floating through Space
by Arthur Ford*

I was critically ill. The doctors said I could not live, but being the good doctors they were, they continued doing what they could. I was in a hospital in Coral Gables, Florida, and my friends had been told that I could not live through the night.

As from a distance, with no feeling except a mild curiosity, I heard a doctor say to a nurse, "Give him the needle; he might as well be comfortable." This I seemed to sense was "it," but I was not afraid. I was simply wondering how long it would take to die.

*Publisher's Note: Arthur Ford is not a member of The Church of Jesus Christ of Latter-day Saints. This account is included to note similarities and contrasts to the other stories included.

Next, I was floating in the air above my bed. I could see my body but had no interest in it. There was a feeling of peace, a sense that all was well.

Now I lapsed into a timeless blank. When I recovered consciousness, I found myself floating through space, without effort, without any sense that I possessed a body as I had known my body. Yet I was myself.

Now there appeared a green valley with mountains on all sides, illuminated everywhere by a brilliance of light and color impossible to describe. People were coming toward me from all around, people I had known and thought of as "dead." I knew them all. Many I had not thought of for years, but it seemed that everyone I had ever cared about was there to greet me.

Recognition was more by personality than by physical attributes. They had changed ages. Some who had passed on in old age were now young, and some who had passed on while children had now matured.

I have often had the experience of traveling to a foreign country, being met by friends and introduced to the local customs and taken to places of interest any visitor to the country would want to see.

It was like that now. Never have I been so royally greeted. I was shown all the things they seemed to think I should see. My memory of these places is as clear as my impression of the countries I have visited in this life. The beauty of a sunrise viewed from a peak in the Swiss Alps, the Blue Grotto of Capri, the hot, dusty roads of India are no more powerfully etched in my memory than the spirit world in which I knew myself to be. Time has never dimmed the memory of it. It is as vivid and real as anything I have ever known.

There was one surprise. Some people I would have expected to see were not present. I asked about them. In the instant of asking, a thin transparent film seemed to fall over my eyes. The light grew dimmer, and colors lost their brilliance. I could no longer see those to whom I had been speaking, but through a haze I saw those for whom I had asked. They, too, were real, but as I looked at them, I felt my own body become heavy. Earthly thoughts crowded into my mind. It was evident to me that I was being shown a lower sphere. I called to them; they seemed to hear me, but I could not hear a reply. Then it was over. A gentle being who looked like a symbol of eternal youth, but radiated power and wisdom, stood by me.

"Don't worry about them," he said. "They can come here whenever they want to if they desire it more than anything else."

Everyone here was busy. They were continually occupied with mysterious errands and seemed to be very happy. Several of those to whom I had been bound by close ties in the past did not seem to be much interested in me. Others I had known only slightly became my companions. I understood that this was right and natural. The law of affinity determined our relationships here.

At some point—I had no awareness of time—I found myself standing before a dazzling white building. Entering, I was told to wait in an enormous anteroom. They said I was to remain here until some sort of disposition had been made of my case. Through wide doors I could glimpse two long tables with people sitting at them and talking—about me.

Guiltily I began an inventory of my life. It did not make a pretty picture. The people at the long tables were also reviewing the record, but the things that worried me did not seem to have much interest for them.

The conventional sins I was warned about as a child were hardly mentioned. But there was sober concern over such matters as selfishness, egotism, stupidity. The word "dissipation" occurred over and over—not in the usual sense of intemperance but as waste of energies, gifts, and opportunities. On the other side of the scale were some simple, kindly things such as we all do from time to time without thinking them of much consequence.

The "judges" were trying to make out the main trend of my life. They mentioned my having failed to accomplish "what he knew he had to finish." There was a purpose for me, it seemed, and I had not fulfilled it. There was a plan for my life, and I had misread the blueprint.

"They're going to send me back," I thought, and I didn't like it. Never did I discover who these people were. They repeatedly used the word "record," perhaps the Akashic Record of the ancient mystic schools—the great universal spiritual sound track on which all events are recorded.

When I was told I had to return to my body, I fought having to go back into that beaten, diseased hulk I had left behind in a Coral Gables hospital. I was standing before a door. I knew if I passed through it, I would be back where I had been. I decided I wouldn't go. Like a spoiled child in a tantrum, I pushed my feet against the wall and fought.

There was a sudden sense of hurtling through space. I opened my eyes and looked into the face of a nurse. I had been in a coma for more than two weeks.

Several things occurred to me as factors which have inhibited my ability to apprehend the realities of the beta (spirit) body and of the expanded universe available to it. Perhaps the most formidable is the misconcept that our five senses—sight, hearing, taste, smell, and touch—are the only means of knowing. . . . It is obvious, if we would only stop and think, that we have many more senses than these.

We see the physical body of the person and some of the kind effects it produces, but the person himself is invisible. Our consciousness resides even now in the same beta (spirit) body it will inhabit in its future journeys. We know people not through the gross five senses but through subtler awarenesses of the beta bodies.

In this sense, speaking from the point of view of the workaday world, we are already invisible and should not be surprised if the actualities of deeply experienced life are not available to our outer eyes and ears.

The beta body can be prepared for its further journey beginning here and now. Character is developed not in the act of dying but in the act of living. Spiritual illumination is no more reached in a single step than is physical perfection or intellectual attainment.

One cannot convince another of the truth of immortality by intellectual arguments or external evidence. It may be known by that inward awareness which is part of every human psyche. It is that awareness which as Wordsworth put it comes as:

A sublime
>   Of something far more deeply interfused. . .
>   A motion and spirit, that impels
>   All thinking things, all objects of all thought,
>   And rolls through all things.

told to Jerome Ellison, The Life Beyond Death,
(New York: G.P. Puttnam's Sons), 1971, pp. 201- 205.

Chapter Ten

A Most Important Work
by Ross Anderson

My wife Nadine was the first to be called to work in the LDS Church genealogy extraction program in our stake. She is an excellent typist. It was the year she retired from her regular job. When she was set apart, we discussed the possibility of me joining her in the work for the dead.

During high school I had been involved in speed typing competitions that were held at Brigham Young University for high schools in the Intermountain area including Idaho, Colorado, and Wyoming. The competitions took place on the stage of the old assembly hall. There was always a large crowd to watch. I was on the team for three years. In the third year, we won the grand prize for having the fastest average typing speed.

In the army I was a court reporter. I took some shorthand and speed-building typing courses, hoping to become a court reporter after getting out of the army. Plans changed, however, and I worked at the Geneva Steel plant in Utah Valley instead.

When they called me to the extraction program, it had been about 35 years since I had done any significant amount of typing. But the minute I sat down at the terminal it was like instant recall. My mind and fingers seemed to surge with energy, and it was like I had never quit typing. I didn't feel the slightest hesitancy. The first afternoon I worked for several hours. The words just flowed across the screen, as easy as could be.

A good, ordinary speed for an extraction typist is 100 to 150 cards per hour. After several months Nadine and I together did 2,000 cards in a four-hour period, all in Spanish. If they kept track of speed, I'm sure that would have been some kind of record.

We had been doing the extraction work about a year when I began feeling ill. I was the high priests group leader in our ward at the time.

It was October 17, 1985, when I had the heart attack. I had been lying around most of the day, feeling very uncomfortable. I took a bath and watched the evening news. We went to bed around 10:30.

About midnight I began thrashing around in bed. Nadine, realizing something was wrong, turned on the bed lamp. Seeing that I was in distress and having trouble breathing, she called the paramedics. They came quickly, but I was dead by the time they arrived. The first one through the door took one look at me and called back to his companions to bring the equipment. They asked Nadine to leave the room as they prepared to give me electric shock treatment. From the other room, she could see my feet flop around every time they applied the electricity.

They rushed me to the hospital where I was on total life support systems for about 30 hours. The doctors wouldn't give Nadine any encouragement about my chances of survival. They made her face the reality that I wasn't going to make it.

Nadine invited our bishop and former bishop in to administer to me. She said it was a strong blessing that indicated I was going to recover.

I have a total memory block covering the next six weeks, except for one experience. I don't remember seeing my body from above or going into a large room or anything like that. But I do remember having a conversation with my older brother, who had died seven years earlier. I can remember the conversation and his face as clearly as anything that has ever happened to me.

I only saw his face and just enough of his body that I could tell he was dressed in white. He was the oldest of the six children in our family. He was the leader, or the spokesman when we did things together. My brother had been on a mission and was always active in the Church. He was the gospel doctrine teacher in his ward in Bountiful at the time of his death.

"Ross," he said, "you are not going to stay here now. You are to return."

Then with added emphasis, he said. "You and Nadine are to continue your work in the extraction center. It's very important that work be done. You are to go back, and you must continue that work."

That was all he said, but I can remember the conversation and his face as clearly as had it happened this morning. I don't remember anything else or any of the background. It was like turning on the TV, then turning it off again. That was all. But it was real, not like a dream.

I was in the hospital about six or seven weeks and then in rehabilitation for about six months before I was able to resume work at the extraction center. Nadine and I have been working there continually for the last three years.

For a while, I experienced a severe memory loss. It took time to begin to recall many things that happened prior to the heart attack. Sometimes I couldn't remember things that happened after the heart attack. I still can't remember those who visited me in the hospital, except my brother and our brief conversation from beyond the veil.

Chapter Eleven

Miracle Baby
by Helen Moffat

Mother used to call me her "miracle baby." In fact, both my older sister and I were placed in that category. The reason goes back to a very special and sacred incident that has been one of our family treasures.

My mother was a small woman. She already had two husky, healthy little boys and had just given birth to a third boy who weighed fourteen pounds at birth.

It was a bleak, February day, nearly ninety years ago that she lay spent and exhausted after many hours of difficult labor. The new little boy lay wrapped in a cradle beside her. As nearly as I can recall her words, this is her account of what happened:

"Suddenly the pain was gone and I felt a sense of comfort and peace that defies description. I opened my eyes and realized that I seemed to be near the ceiling with the room and its contents below me.

"A presence was urging me on, but I could not tear myself away. I felt I must stay and somehow give comfort to the weeping people near the bed. I was shocked to realize it was me lying there so still, with my beloved husband kneeling by my side, his face buried in my outstretched hand, and his shoulders shaking with sobs. On the other side of the bed another man, the doctor, held my wrist in his fingers. Then he gently placed my hand on the coverlet, turned to the woman beside him and said, 'She's gone.' My mother and two sisters stood with their arms locked together for support against the weight of their grief.

"The urging of the unseen presence became more insistent. The scene below seemed to fade as if I had gone beyond the room. I found myself pleading with all my power to be allowed to remain to raise my sons and support my husband. I was saying there was so much more for me to do, that my time could not be finished.

"A great stillness came over me. I looked down and could see the room once more. The doctor had stepped to the door and my mother had moved to the cradle to pick up my infant son.

"Like a shock the mantle of pain enveloped my body again. I heard my husband cry out as my hand moved against his face. I realized my pleas had been heard and my desires granted."

Seven years after this incident my sister was born and I joined the family five years after that. My mother lived to be sixty-four years of age. Her life was one of devotion to her family, love and compassion for all who knew her, and continuous service to her Lord through positions and assignments in the Church.

Since I have been old enough to realize the significance of this event, it has been a strength to me and a reinforcement of my knowledge and testimony that God lives, loves us, and answers our prayers. I am so grateful that the Lord saw fit to let me be a "miracle baby" by allowing my mother to return from beyond the veil.

Chapter Twelve

Mary, Mary Quite Contrary
by Mary McGary

My patriarchal blessing says that I was privileged to help plan my life on earth, "blessed with choice earthly parentage."

I was named Mary because I was born a short time before Christmas. Mother called me a strong-willed child. She said once I made up my mind about something, I did not easily change it to a contrary opinion. While growing up I was often called, "Mary, Mary, quite contrary."

After my older sister, Lisa, was born, Mother did not get well as quickly as she should have. For five months she struggled with poor health. She and father decided that perhaps seven children was enough. They felt she didn't have the strength to endure another pregnancy.

One night a woman appeared to Mother in a dream.

"Your little girl wants you to come and get her," the woman said.

Mother thought of all her children, one by one, then told the woman that her children were all in bed. The woman did not argue.

"She says she's your little girl," the woman said. Then in the dream Mother and Father decided to get the little girl. Their hearts were filled with joy. The dream ended.

Mother did not attach any meaning to the dream at first, but it stayed in her mind for several days. Finally she told Father about it.

"Maybe there's another little girl for us," he said, simply.

A short time later Mother found out she was going to have another baby. She knew it was going to be a girl. Instead of feeling like she didn't have the strength to go through another pregnancy, she awaited my coming with great joy and anticipation, knowing I was the little girl who had asked to come to them.

Later, Mother said that pregnancy and my birth were as easy if not easier than any of the others. And though my mother has gone beyond the veil, I realize that our connection to the spirit world is very close.

Chapter Thirteen

She Was A Great and Noble Spirit
by Cathy Anderegg

My fifth child, Angeline, now age five is very strong-willed. From the time she was a tiny infant she has been very difficult, super-sensitive to her environment, and very demanding. She is very sure about what she wants, and very determined to get it. In those times when I am frustrated with her, I am so grateful for a special experience that happened at the time of Angeline's birth.

After experiencing a very routine pregnancy, and a routine four hours of beginning labor, it was finally time to enter the delivery room and bring the new baby into the world. I was wheeled into the room and transferred to the delivery table. I had already had four successful births and should have been taking this one in stride. But I was as excited about this birth as any of the others. The process had not yet become routine. I was very nervous and even a little frightened. I remember I was trembling all over.

Then something happened that I don't recall happening at any of the other births. For about two or three minutes, everyone but me left the delivery room. The doctor went to scrub. The nurse went to get some supplies. My husband was outside putting on a sterile gown.

I was all alone in that white, sterile, metallic, and rather cold room. My trembling increased. I closed my eyes and thought about the baby to come. Our first baby had been a beautiful, sweet girl. The next three babies were noisy, rough-and-tumble boys. I longed for another sweet, gentle, quiet girl and wondered if it would ever again be possible.

Suddenly I saw a tall, dark-haired woman standing just to my right. She leaned over me and put her arm around my shoulder. I felt a great feeling of affection and knew she was trying to comfort me and calm my fears and trembling. I had the impression that she would be a great help and comfort to me during my life and that she was a great and noble spirit.

The woman disappeared as the others began coming back into the room, followed shortly by the birth of an adorable dark-haired baby girl. I knew the minute I saw that dark hair that my new baby girl was the woman who had stood by me moments earlier.

Angeline is now very blonde, and at most times, not much of a comfort. And it is when I stand confronting a pouting, foot-stamping little girl that I am reminded of the special, close time we shared as mature spiritual equals just prior to her entrance into this mortal world. I am thankful the Lord allowed the veil to be thin at that time, and I look forward to sharing my life with this wonderful spirit—if I can just get her past the childhood years.

I've often thought how profitable it would be for all mothers to be able to see, just for a moment, the great spiritual potential of their children. We would probably be a lot more compassionate, patient, and respectful towards them and realize that those childhood years do not last forever.

Chapter Fourteen

I Persuaded the Messenger
to Let Me Return
by Carlos Hjorth

In the fall of 1955, our company was preparing curved sections of pipe for the Pioneer Products Pipe Line Company which was working on a pipeline connecting the Sinclair, Wyoming, oil fields with the Salt Lake refineries. We were fabricating the pipe at our shop in Mapleton, Utah.

One October morning the inspectors from the oil company were on hand to make sure the pipe met specifications. I was there with a truck to pick up another load of pipe. We were pulling a steel ball through the new sections of pipe. If the ball could pass through, the inspectors knew the pipe would allow their cleaning instrument, called the pig, to pass through the line after the pipe was installed.

As I watched this process I noticed the winch lugging up and the steel cable getting unusually tight. I decided to get out of the way.

As I turned to leave, one of the pulleys broke. A piece of steel struck me in the back, crushing eleven ribs and turning a portion of my liver to mush. I was knocked about 15 feet out into the yard. Still conscious, I realized I was going to die. Instead of feeling panic or fear, I remember thinking that finally I was going to find out what it was like on the other side. I was waiting to experience death. Though I was very curious about what was going to happen next, I didn't want to die. I kept thinking about my wife and five children. The youngest, Charles, was only four months old at the time.

The next thing I remember was my brother Hugh pushing an oxygen hose in my nose and mouth. Somehow I managed to tell him I wanted a priesthood blessing. Bishop Harold Harmer from Payson had just arrived in a delivery truck. He assisted my good friend Freeman Bird, who had been helping me load pipe, in giving me the blessing.

I have been administered to many times in my life and have usually forgotten what was said. But this blessing I remember. Freeman promised me, by the power of the priesthood, that I would live. He said I would have a lot of pain, and it would take my body a long time to heal, but I would live.

I remember the ambulance ride to Utah Valley Hospital in Provo. Every time we hit a bump or turned a corner I felt like I was being run over by a truck. My brother, Hugh, was leaning over me, crying. I tried to tell him everything would be all right, but I was so far in shock by that time that I couldn't speak.

I remember being rushed into surgery and needles being pushed into my feet. I unsuccessfully tried to tell the doctors they wouldn't need to use anesthetic to put me to sleep because I could no longer feel anything.

It was some time during the first 12 hours following the injury that I remember awakening and getting out of bed. It was like I was just getting up to go home. But when I glanced back at the bed I saw my body was still there.

I don't remember a tunnel or a bright light or anything like that, only that I found myself in one of the most pleasant, busy places one can imagine. I was standing before what appeared to be a fog bank or veil. Several people in white flowing robes were going to and from the fog. One of them approached me to become my escort. I did not recognize this individual.

"No, no," I said, my voice loud, almost shouting. I knew what was happening and I didn't want to be part of it, not yet. I explained that I had been promised in a priesthood blessing that I would continue living. I begged for 20 more years so I could help my wife raise our young family. I promised to spend the remainder of my days on earth serving in the Church and helping build the kingdom.

The messenger reminded me that if I returned to my body I would have to endure much suffering. The healing process would be very difficult. I told him that was agreeable to me. The next thing I knew I was back in my room at the hospital. Getting back into my body was as easy as getting back into bed.

I spent the next 70 days in the hospital and had to return on a frequent basis for about five years. Sometimes I wondered how a person could endure so much pain. While in the hospital I had tubes coming from my abdomen and back which the doctor pulled back and forth to break the abscesses on the liver. I would go back into surgery several times a week where the doctor would spread my ribs apart so he could reach into my back with his hand to massage the liver and break up the abscesses.

I spent a lot of time pondering the pain, always wondering how much more I could endure. I felt very close to my Savior at this time. Because of my suffering, I often pondered the great suffering he had to go through for our sins, in the garden and on the cross. Those months in the hospital were a strengthening and mellowing experience for me. I felt a great peace in my soul and believed I was in the presence of administering angels who were encouraging me to accept my suffering.

It was a full month after the accident, at Thanksgiving, that the doctor finally told my family that he thought I might recover. My wife came to see me every day. I got to where I could tell she was coming by the click of her heels. My parents came home from their mission in California to see me. I remember looking out my window and seeing them get out of their car and wondering why they had come home and then realizing that there was still concern on the part of the doctors and my family that I might not survive.

Slowly I began to heal. At Christmas they allowed me to go home to my family. Every night I went to sleep counting my blessings.

Not only was I given the 20 years I asked for to help my wife raise our children, but another 13 on top of that. I sometimes wonder about that priesthood blessing the day of the accident wherein Freeman Bird promised that I would live. Had he not said those words I don't think I would have been allowed to return from beyond the veil.

Chapter Fifteen

Nobody Believed Me
by Jean Scott

My husband, Dave, was in the graduate school of engineering at BYU in the late sixties. We had two little girls, and I was pregnant with our third child.

One Sunday evening I began hemorrhaging, a little at first, but then it became serious. Dave had to keep bringing me fresh towels as the old ones became soggy with blood. He ran to the nearest pay phone to call the doctor who wasn't in, but the lady taking the calls told Dave to give me paregoric.

The bleeding continued until we decided we had better go to the hospital. When I tried to get out of bed I passed out, collapsing onto the floor. Dave dragged me into the kitchen. I remember feeling cold, but calm, as Dave tried to revive me.

About this time my sister stopped by. She was on the way home from church and wanted to see how I was doing. Upon seeing me on the kitchen floor, she screamed. She sent Dave to get a registered nurse who lived across the street. While at the nurse's house, he called for an ambulance.

The nurse could see by the way my eyes were dilating that I was going into shock. She wrapped me in blankets. By the time the ambulance arrived, I was feeling much better, though I still felt cold.

The doctor met me at the hospital. At first our conversation was casual.

"What have you been doing?" he asked.

"Bleeding all over the house," I responded.

I suppose he didn't take me serious, because it wasn't until the nurse took my blood pressure that he became very earnest.

"You didn't tell me you were bleeding," he shouted. "We've got to go into surgery immediately."

He began swearing when he discovered the lights were off and the door locked in surgery. It was late.

Twenty minutes later I found myself on the operating table. Because of my low blood level, I was informed I would not be receiving any anesthetic. The doctor was preparing to perform a D&C (dilation and curetage).

I remember how painful it was as the doctor went to work. For the first time I felt terror. I was afraid to die. The next thing I remember was the voice of the nurse.

"Doctor, her breathing has stopped," she said.

"Doctor, her pulse is gone," she added.

I felt my spirit kind of gathering to the middle of my body, then draining out the back. I found myself in the corner of the room, floating in mid-air, watching the doctor and nurses trying to revive the body on the operating table.

I felt like I could go back to my body but didn't want to. Suddenly I was aware of a dark tunnel, like a doorway leaving the operating room. I could see it, but the doctor and nurses couldn't.　Though I was afraid, I entered the tunnel and found myself traveling very fast towards the far end. I wasn't walking or running, just floating along, very fast. There was a light at the end of the tunnel. It wasn't a blue light, but a warm golden light, very bright. As I neared the end of the tunnel it became very narrow, but I made it through, finding myself in an open place with other people. I recognized two of them, my grandfather, Leo Bowers whom I had known as a little girl, and my great-grandfather, Richard Britton, whom I had been doing some genealogy work for. Both of them were very glad to see me.

The glowing personage who had been the light at the end of the tunnel told me I had to go back. He said no one else could raise my little girls for me. He said my life would be hard, but he would be with me. This communication didn't seem to be with words. Thoughts just passed back and forth.

Somehow I felt cheated that I was not being allowed to stay with the rest of the people around me. I still didn't want to go back.

The next thing I remember was the doctor hitting me in the face, very hard.

"Listen to me," he said, forcefully. "You are not leaving this room as long as I am here."

The next day he told me the reason he had struck me and spoken so forcefully was because he could see that I was gone, and he sensed that I didn't want to come back.

On several occasions I tried to tell people what had happened, but I was rebuffed. They thought I had been hallucinating or that the loss of blood had caused brain damage. Even my husband didn't want me to tell anyone what had happened.

As a result, I kept the experience to myself for many years, though I continued to think a lot about what had happened. I became obsessed with the meaning of life and experiencing the most life could offer. I began reading a lot. I remembered the messenger's promise that he would be with me. Though I have never seen his face again or heard his voice, I have felt that same quiet, confident communication when I have been seeking solutions to life's difficult problems.

Against the doctors' advice, I became pregnant four more times, losing two of the babies prematurely, coming near death again with another of the pregnancies. I knew that several of the people I had seen at the end of the tunnel were to be my future children, so I continued getting pregnant until I felt I had brought them into the world. I am no longer afraid of death after my experience beyond the veil.

Chapter Sixteen

He Begged for Forgiveness
by Judy Jackson

I had been ill for seven or eight years, to the point where I was totally bedfast. I was not able to walk or take care of my family in any manner or even turn over in bed. I was dying. None of my doctors could find out what the problem was.

I found out somewhere along the way that before I was born my father had tried to get my mother to have an abortion. I had been treated very cruelly by my father after I was born, but I had always tried to please him.

I was five and a half years old when my parents were divorced. My mother never told me anything good about my father. I usually saw him about once a year after the divorce, around the time of my birthday. He usually spent the time trying to convince me to come and live with him and his new wife. It was a terrible conflict, wanting to trust him, and love him, but not being able to do it.

My father worked in a service station most of the time that I remember, and later he worked pouring concrete. I was the oldest of three children he had by my mother. He had four children by his second wife.

I had very low self-esteem. Later in life, as I became ill, I realized somewhere in my subconscious mind that I was ill because I was trying to kill myself to please my father.

Each year when the farmers started spraying the orchards, I would become even sicker. It seemed I was allergic to everything, but when the spraying began I simply couldn't exist. I had degenerated to the point that when they started spraying this particular spring, I knew I would not be able to survive the season. I became very concerned about being ready to meet my Father in Heaven when I died, and I spent several days with this in my mind and prayers.

Finally, I was told that it was necessary for me to forgive my earthly father. I tried for several days but just couldn't do it. I couldn't force myself to have feelings that just didn't exist, even though my father had been dead for about 15 years.

One day when I was alone in the house, my father and his father (my grandfather) suddenly appeared in my room. My father was standing above the head of the bed, and my grandfather was at the foot of the bed. I felt surrounded. I had to bend my head back to see my father.

As soon as they appeared, I was frightened, and began screaming at my grandfather to get my father out of the room. I was hysterical. Then I screamed at my father, telling him to leave. I reminded him of all the things he had done to me and how much he had hurt me, and continued screaming hysterically for him to leave.

My grandfather had a very calm, loving, and patient look in his eyes. Eventually, my father came around to the foot of the bed beside my grandfather. My father told me he was being held back in his progression because of the hate and contempt I felt for him. He said that was the reason for the visit.

My father had never been active in the Church. He had smoked and used tobacco all his life, even though he and mother had been married in the temple. My grandfather had always been active and had been a great missionary. He had spent 15 years as a missionary in Alaska. I'm sure he had been working very hard with Father.

My father told me that he could not progress until I forgave him. He said that it was not anything I had done that caused him to treat me the way he did. He said his behavior towards me was the result of some things he had done, especially when he was a teenager. As a result he had hated himself. He hadn't wanted any children because he was afraid they would grow up and become like him. He said he didn't think I had remembered all the things he had done to me. I could see the tears running down his face as he asked—no pleaded—for me to forgive him. After this last communication, he and my grandfather disappeared.

For the next four or five days a purging process went on in my mind and body. I told several people about the experience, wrote things in my journal, and continued to pray.

At the end of that time, the hatred and contempt and fear of my father, which had been penned up inside me for so many years, seemed to be totally gone. I was actually looking forward to seeing my father again in the next world and being close to him as his child.

As I understand the gospel, sealings occur by the power of the priesthood and are confirmed by the Holy Spirit of Promise. I also believe that love and forgiveness are part of the sealing process. I learned this the day my father came from beyond the veil to ask me for my forgiveness.

Chapter Seventeen

The Personage Had a Body
by John Lauderdale

At age five I came down with a severe case of Bright's Disease. I was in the hospital in Muskogee, Oklahoma, and was going into my third week with no kidney function. The doctors were getting ready to fly me to Oklahoma City. They believed the only way to keep me alive was to put me on a kidney machine but were reluctant to do so knowing I would be dependent upon that machine for the rest of my life. This was before the days of organ transplants. It was 1955.

The night prior to the plane trip to Oklahoma City, my parents were seated beside my bed in the hospital room. I was partially blinded from the continuous high fever. I was in a lot of pain, too. Neither I nor my parents belonged to the LDS Church so I had not been administered to, though several of the local Protestant churches had held prayer meetings in my behalf.

Suddenly the room became very bright. A man dressed in white was standing in the air beside my bed. He said he had come to take me home. I could see him clearly in the bright light. My blindness was gone.

My mother and father could not see or hear the visitor, so I told them I was going home. At first they didn't understand, thinking I meant my earthly home. I told them Jesus was standing beside my bed and had come to take me home. My mother began to cry thinking I was going to die. She and my father began to pray.

At the time I thought it was Jesus who was appearing to me, but now I am not so sure. I had been shown pictures of Jesus in white robes in Sunday School and just assumed it was him. It could have been someone else. I just know I was visited by a heavenly messenger.

Suddenly my kidneys began passing blood, then urine. The fever broke, and the pain disappeared. I was no longer delirious. The personage disappeared. The room became dark, but I could see. My eyesight was restored. My kidneys were functioning again. The trip to Oklahoma City was no longer necessary.

The next day my parents decided to devote their lives to serving the Lord. My father, however, strayed from that path and died a terrible death through alcohol abuse. My mother has remained a devout member of the Baptist Church.

As for me, I had trouble being very devout in any church. After seeing the heavenly being, I had trouble accepting what the churches taught about God, Jesus, and the Holy Ghost being one big spirit. The personage I had seen had had a body, perhaps not a mortal body of flesh and blood like mine, but a body just the same. I discussed the subject with several ministers but could never get any satisfaction.

I first learned about the Mormons in junior high school, in a book about Jim Bridger. I didn't begin studying the doctrine until I was 20. When the missionaries told me about heavenly beings having resurrected bodies of flesh and bone, I knew that doctrine was true. I joined the Church at 23. My wife, Beth, was already a member, and I had been attending with her for several years.

I sometimes think back on that experience in the hospital, wondering why my life was spared, why I was visited by a heavenly messenger. I believe I was allowed to live for good reason, perhaps so I could be with my wife Beth and our five children. With time I think I will know more.

Chapter Eighteen

Impossible Things Just Take Longer
by Neddie Pitcher

As I go over the happenings of the past few years, I know I must write them down. Perhaps others, after reading this, will find additional strength for the tests and trials in their lives. One thing I have learned is that no matter how long or how hard life sometimes is or however long the storm might last, there is always a rainbow in the end. With trust in the Lord, we can learn and grow from each of life's storms.

That morning in July, 1984, was sunny and beautiful. My husband, Vern, and I finished packing, said good-bye to our six children and two grandchildren, loaded our suitcases in the car, and were off to the Denver airport. What excitement! We were going to Europe, a vacation we had been planning for a long time.

Our first destination was Frankfurt, where our good friends Dick and Nancy Wright were going to meet us. Dick had taken time off from work so he and Nancy could show us Europe.

After a twelve-hour flight and a day's time change, we landed in Frankfurt. It was a tearful reunion. We hadn't seen Dick and Nancy for almost three years.

They lived in Dizenbach, a suburb of Frankfurt. The road went through a forest of tall, green trees. Everywhere I looked there was lush greenery. We stopped at a little flower stand where Dick bought some flowers.

That night I had a hard time sleeping. I suppose it was excitement about being in Germany, but also there was the return of a premonition of danger that I had felt back in Colorado. I tried to push the feeling out of my mind, finally falling to sleep about 3 a.m.

The next day we began our tour of Germany. Many of the towns had cobblestone streets and quaint little shops. The roofs of the homes were covered with red tile, and the children played in lederhosen. Our travels included Dizenbach, a cruise down the Rhine River where we saw 28 castles in 29 miles, Kobleinz, Rutersheim, Munich, Dinkelsbuhl, Heidelburg, Rothenburg, Chemese, and finally Berchesgarten.

As we traveled, we stayed with the people of the country so we could get more of a feel for the places we were visiting. If someone had a room for rent they would have a sign that read, "Zimmerfrie," which translated means, "Room for rent."

Just as we entered Berchesgarten, Dick spotted a road that led up into the mountains and turned onto it. We climbed a very steep hill, wondering if the car would be able to make the climb. Upon reaching the top, we entered the most beautiful valley I have ever seen. In the middle was a house with a sign that read "Zimmerfrie." We could hardly believe our good luck. Dick and Vern arranged for us to stay two nights.

The valley was rich and green. There was a small stream flowing through the open meadows just below the house. In front of the house was a hand-carved water trough and a pump with faces on them. Across the street from the house was a green pasture with sheep and cattle grazing. Behind the house, the mountain went straight up. At the top and to the right a little was Hitler's Eagle Nest retreat. The house we were staying in had been in our host's family for 600 years.

That afternoon we took a boat across a lake to King Ludwig's castle, followed by dinner at a restaurant in Berchesgarten. We left the restaurant about 9 p.m. It was beginning to rain. I remember feeling those premonitions of danger again but brushed them aside.

I took hold of Vern's hand, and we started across the street. The traffic light had been turned off, so we looked both ways before crossing. We had decided to call the children in Colorado, and the only phone was at the Bonn Hoff, the old train station that once belonged to Hitler.

As we reached the far side of the street one of my shoes fell off. We were just stepping onto the curb when I let go of Vern's hand and stepped back into the street to get my shoe. That's the last thing I remember. I was hit by a car. I was killed instantly. It was 9:10 p.m., July 28, 1984.

I don't remember being hit, but I do remember standing above my body and watching what was going on. Vern had not seen the car hit me. He only heard the thud of my body hitting the car, and the headlight glass breaking.

He turned, screaming my name, looking for me under the car. But I wasn't there. The car had hit me in the left leg just below the hip, flipping me onto the hood, then as it came to a stop, pitching me forward a few feet. I landed on my head, according to the report of a witness. Vern found me lying on the wet street. He called to Dick and Nancy.

They ran to me. There was blood all over. Vern gathered me up in his arms. He was screaming,

"They've killed my baby. They've killed my baby." Dick tried to console him, but Vern was hysterical by this time. Nancy ran across the street to call an ambulance.

People came from all over to see what they could do to help. There was a language problem. They gathered up my things that had been thrown all over the street, then waited around in the event there was something else they might do.

Dick put my head in his hands and—even though there were no vital signs and he knew I was dead—gave me a blessing. He later told me he felt prompted by the Spirit to do so.

I remember trying to reach out to Vern to comfort him, but I couldn't do it. I left the scene of the accident at this point and traveled through a gray mist that became lighter as I traveled upward. Eventually the fog gave way to brilliant light as I entered a beautiful garden. I don't have words to describe the beauty of the garden, more beautiful than anything I had ever seen on earth, including the Koukenhoff Garden in Holland at tulip time.

I was looking for my grandmother, because I knew she would be there to greet me, but I was alone in the garden.

"My daughter, what are you doing here?" asked a voice from behind. I turned and saw a man in white whose radiance and love astonished me. He was standing in a group of trees. He began moving towards me. As he spoke, and as I felt the love and light that radiated from him, I believed he was my Father in Heaven.

He told me that I must return to earth and be with my family and to put my family together again. He told me other things which I cannot repeat and also that I would know my mission in life as time went on. When I re-entered my body, it was in the ambulance on the way to the hospital.

A young policeman took Vern to the hospital, and Dick and Nancy came in their car. When Vern arrived, the doctors came out and asked Vern if he wanted to see the x-rays of his wife before they took her into surgery. Vern didn't know what they were talking about. He thought I was dead. He didn't know my spirit had re-entered my body in the ambulance.

The doctors then took Vern to me. I was talking to the doctors, but I don't remember this or anything else that happened for the next six weeks, except for the nightmares.

I had a ruptured spleen which was removed two days after the accident. My back was broken in two places. My pelvis was crushed and broken in four places. They said my insides looked like scrambled eggs. I was paralyzed from the waist down. Later, I lost muscle control of my arms. There was a five-inch cut on my head and a large hematoma by my right eye, causing pressure on the brain resulting in a cerebral contusion. Two days after the accident my lungs collapsed. I took over 30 pints of blood, had five major surgeries in seven weeks, was on life support for three and a half weeks after that, and was kept unconscious for six weeks. I almost lost my right kidney.

Four doctors and six nurses never left me from the time I was brought into the hospital in Berchesgarten until I left two days later for a larger hospital in Salzburg, Austria, where I spent the next two months.

At the hospital in Berchesgarten, the doctors did two surgeries to see what organ was bleeding so badly, but since everything inside me was in such a mess, they couldn't tell where the bleeding was coming from. Since it was my spleen that was ruptured, all the blood they pumped into me just bled inside my body, swelling me up like a blimp.

When my lungs collapsed two days after the accident, Vern was at the police station filling out reports. The doctors immediately put me on a life support system, loaded me in an ambulance, and with one doctor riding with me, sent me to a large trauma and intensive care unit in Salzburg. When Vern returned to the hospital, the doctor came out and said, "She's gone." With his limited understanding of German, Vern at first thought I had died. Dick and Nancy picked up Vern and our things and headed for Salzburg.

When they arrived at the hospital, I had been in surgery again and the spleen had been removed. I was finally stabilizing. When they let Vern into the room where I was recovering from the surgery, along with several other patients, Vern had to ask which one was me. I was so blue and swollen from all the internal bleeding that he didn't recognize me. When he saw me it made him sick, and he had to leave. He told Dick and Nancy he couldn't stand to see me like that.

The doctors never gave him much hope that I would live. I was too broken up, and if I did live, they thought I would be paralyzed and have brain damage.

A week after the accident, Dick and Nancy went home, and our 15-year-old daughter Marnie came to Austria so Vern would not be alone. She stayed a month.

When Vern and Marnie came each day to the hospital, they would encourage me to fight for my life, to say my prayers, and to come back to them. Marnie would rub my legs and arms so that hopefully some life would come back into them. I don't remember any of this, still being unconscious. I only remember the last several days of Marnie's visit before she had to return to Colorado.

I remember waking up at nights and not remembering where I was. I could see shadows of people and flashing lights and hear weird sounds and a foreign language. I had a nightmare that I had been kidnapped.

I was sharing a ward with 12 other people who were also badly broken up. I was the only one of the original 12 to survive.

I would have this dream of being on a ship of some kind, of it wrecking and then being in some kind of a shed all alone. I couldn't use my legs, and I was very afraid. Then I would hear someone coming, and I would call out in my dream for Heavenly Father to give me strength to face whatever was ahead of me. I then would wake up not knowing where I was, but feeling Father's presence. I would shiver, and one of my monitors would go off, and someone would come and take my hand. Then I would feel His presence leave, and the nurse would give me something to sleep again. This happened several times, the same dream and the same happenings. Even after I came to my senses, six weeks later, the nightmares continued until I came home.

I got very close to my intensive care nurse, Ursula. On her days off I didn't do as well as when she was there. She was always encouraging me to do things. Whenever I would wake up from a nap and not fully remember where I was, she would be there holding my hand and saying everything was okay. Before I came home she gave me a stick pin of a guardian angel, and we still write back and forth.

Another woman I got very close to was the cleaning lady in the intensive care unit. One day as I awakened, she was cleaning off my bed. She smiled at me and I back to her. Each time I would see her I would smile and she back. Then one day she took my hand and kissed it and touched my cheek. She was from Yugoslavia, speaking no English and very little German. Of course, I didn't speak her language.

We communicated through touch, smiles, and lots of love. When she would finish her day's work, she would scrub up and come back to my bed and rub my arms and legs for me. We became the very best of friends, without words. I taught her the international sign for "I love you." Each night as she left to go home she would come to the door, and we would sign it to each other.

One of my friends had sent me a stuffed mouse for my birthday, but since I was in a semi-conscious state at the time, Vern kept it to show me when I was fully conscious. After coming to my senses, I wouldn't believe the doctors or nurses or Vern or Marnie that I was in a hospital and very badly hurt. It was then that Vern brought me the mouse and showed it to me. I was able to get my arms up and grab hold of it, and I held it very tight to my chest. This was the first time anyone had seen me cry. Things were finally starting to make sense to me.

Ursula took the mouse from me, tied a string to the bow on its head and tied it on the bar above my bed. It was the only thing permitted in the intensive care unit that wasn't scrubbed and polished. It went everywhere with me except surgery. My cleaning lady took hold of it one day, and I told her I collected mice, and she seemed to understand. She would talk in her language, and I in mine, and we got long just fine. We became the best of friends.

Each morning several doctors came in to see how I was doing and how I felt. They would gather around my bed and would ask if I had any pain. I don't remember any pain until the day after they did the surgery to save my kidney.

One morning when the doctors came in they all had very serious looks on their faces. I asked what was wrong. I remember that I was smiling at them as I did every time they came in. One of the doctors took hold of my hand and told me that I would never be able to walk, that my left foot had come back to normal position, but that my right foot hadn't, and that because of the nerve damage it was most likely that it never would.

I smiled at him and put my other hand over his and said it was all right. As I looked up into his eyes, a tear had formed and was on his cheek. He squeezed my hand and said, "I don't understand. I just told you that you were never going to walk again, and you're telling me it's all right? Your husband has told us how active you were, and you're smiling at us and saying it's okay?"

I looked up at him and at the other doctors and said, "I'm alive, and that's all that matters."

I told the doctors that I had told my family many times that if I had to lose a part of my body and if I had a choice, it would be my legs because if I had my hands I would still be able to do the things that I loved to do, such as hand sewing, ceramics, and crafts.

"I just don't understand you," one of the doctors said. "You're smiling and telling us it's okay that you'll never walk again. Don't you ever stop smiling?"

I don't think I realized how badly I had been hurt until the morning some nurses came in and said they needed to sit me up as I was not getting the circulation in my legs that I needed. I didn't think it would be any big deal, but I was very wrong. I couldn't sit up, at least not by myself. It took all four of the nurses to hold me up. I was like a wet noodle. It was at that moment that I finally believed what the doctors and nurses had tried to tell me, that I had been very seriously injured.

Dick, Nancy, and Vern had decided to tell me I had had a bad fall, not to let me know I had been killed and then had come back to life, but they quickly gave up on that when I began telling them exactly what each one of them had said and done immediately following the accident. It was the first time any of them realized I had an out-of-body experience.

I never felt angry or bitter that the accident had happened. I was alive, and I was determined to be the best person I could no matter the circumstances. I was sent back to earth for a reason, and I was determined to do my best at whatever it was He wanted me to do.

Life, what a beautiful and precious gift! Why do we take it for granted? I know I did before my accident but not anymore. Each day is beautiful and exciting because I am alive to enjoy it. I love the sunrise, the sunset. I watch the birds as they come to the feeder. I watch the little ants as they carry home their loads. I take each day as it comes. I don't live by hours and minutes or seconds anymore. Just day and night, and I am grateful for each new day. I am so grateful for the little things I can do with my hands, like write my name.

After several months in the hospital, I was getting very homesick for my children. I wanted to go home. The doctors kept saying that I couldn't go until I was strong enough to sit up for long periods of time. It was a 13-hour flight home. They said that sitting up that long in my present condition would kill me.

One night as I lay awake, I decided that come September 25th I was going home, no matter what, even if I had to crawl. I told Vern the next morning. He wanted to go home, too, so he said he would see what he could do. With Dick's help he found out Delta had a sleeper jet where I could lay down in flight. He reported his find to the doctors, who agreed to let me go provided I would work very hard to strengthen myself for the trip.

I had to work with rings hanging over my bed three times a day to strengthen my arms. I was taken out of bed to practice walking at least twice a day. Physical therapy sessions were increased to four times a day. These sessions included painful electric shock treatments to stimulate feeling in my legs.

The doctors, nurses, and others from the intensive care unit called nearly every day to see how I was and what I had accomplished that day. Everyone in the ward encouraged me to do better. There were lots of tears, hugs, and promises.

We exchanged tapes with the children and other family members in Colorado and Utah. My voice was low with a gravelly sound, hard for the children to understand, but there was a lot I wanted to say. Sometimes as we go through life we say and do things that hurt others, and we let those words or deeds build up and won't forget them. I don't know why it is so hard to ask for forgiveness or to apologize. Hurt feelings and hate become like cancer—eating away at our hearts. I know now that with love we can conquer anything. With love, we can forgive and be forgiven.

One night we were in the hallway waiting for a call from the children. I was lying in the wheelchair, and Vern was talking to the nurses. A little lady in her eighties came down the hall with her crutches. We smiled at one another as we did every day in the hallway as we both were learning to use our crutches. I put my hand on hers and smiled. I had the nurse tell her that I was going home in a few days. The woman got tears in her eyes, and I put my arms around her neck and kissed her cheek. She said she must go to her room, and so I said good-bye to her and wished her well.

In a while the little lady returned to my wheelchair. She handed me a two-inch square picture of the Virgin Mary. I looked at it and started to hand it back to her, but she shook her head and pushed my hand away.

The picture was well-worn and wrinkled, and I knew it had a special meaning to her. In German, she said that over ten years ago she had gone on a pilgrimage to where the Virgin Mary was supposed to have appeared to someone in a vision or something like that and that while there everyone received a picture. She had carried it in her wallet all this time, but she wanted to give it to me now.

I thought I couldn't possibly take this possession that meant so much to her. With tears in my eyes and a lump in my throat, I told the nurse to tell her that I was very touched by her gift, but that I didn't want to take it since it meant so much to her. The little lady pushed the picture back in my hands and turned it over. In German she had written, "God bless you and your family."

Gratefully I accepted her picture. I carry it in my wallet, as she did. Every time I see it I remember a special night of love and friendship between two people who could not even understand one another, but through love we became friends. I never saw her again, but I know we will meet in the eternities, and we will be the best of friends.

A few days before we left for home, Vern took me in my wheelchair and we visited all the people in the intensive care unit to say good-bye. We took pictures and hugged and kissed them—doctors, nurses, staff, and my little cleaning lady. It was a tearful good-bye, but I promised that I would be back, and when I came, I would walk through the doors to see them.

I had mixed emotions about going home. I wanted to go back to my family, but I would be leaving a big part of my heart in Austria. Sleep was a long time in coming that night.

I wanted to go home, and yet I didn't. I never thought it would be so hard to leave a hospital, but the doctors and nurses who had taken care of me had become very good friends. It was hard to say good-bye to them. I thanked each one for the good care they had given me and for all the help they had been to us while we were in Austria. All of them went far beyond their required duty.

We flew first to Frankfurt, where we spent the night with Dick and Nancy, then we boarded the flight for home. We changed flights in Dallas, then headed for Denver.

I had to wait until all the other passengers had gotten off and then a young man came to assist me in the wheelchair. He pushed me down the long aisle toward the room where the kids would be waiting.

All at once at the door appeared our little granddaughter, Jacki Sue. "Grandma," she screamed as she came running to us. She threw her arms around my neck and hung onto me. I held her little hand as we went up the aisle to the doorway where the rest of the family was waiting. Everyone was there, except our son Marc who had a football game in Pueblo that night. He sent a note, hoping we would understand his absence. It was so good to see all of them again and to feel their arms around my neck. I had been so homesick for them.

The next few months were busy and happy. Friends and loved ones came by to visit or help around the house.

Each time I was able to do something for myself, tears of gratitude fell. It was so exciting to be able to once again do those things that I thought I would never do again like feed myself without spilling food in my lap, brushing my own teeth, being able to comb my hair and then one day even dressing myself.

Two days before Halloween I walked by myself to the living room. There was no stopping me now. Vern had sold my car thinking I would never drive again, but by January he had to get me another one.

I still have only partial feeling in my right leg, and it still has nerve damage. I have no feeling in my left leg where I was hit, but I walk. I can even run, not fast, but run. And I have gone back to racquetball. I can't play as fast as I once did, but at least I'm back on the court. My right eye becomes very blurry at times, and I have my aches and pains, but that's not serious. I'm alive.

Goals have become a very important part of my life. I believe that all righteous goals are attainable with God's help. I no longer believe in depression. I have found a joy and happiness in myself and a peace within myself that I have never had before.

My test wasn't the injuries I received in the accident or the hardships I have had to overcome. My test was how I accepted what had happened to me. I believe I had already accepted it before I came to earth.

One night as I was saying my prayers and thanking my Father in Heaven for all the blessings He had given me and for the miracles that had come into my life, a small voice came to me and said, "It really doesn't matter what your trials or tests may be here on earth. It's how you accept them. That's the real test."

I was asked once at a fireside if I would change anything that's happened these past few years. My answer was no. I thought once that if I could change the pain and agony that loved ones and friends went through while I was in Europe I would change that. But the more I thought about it, I realized that perhaps that time was a test for them, too. I would not change anything. It's been the greatest thing that has ever happened to me. I am not the same person that I was two years ago.

Some mornings it would be a lot easier to stay in bed because those first steps hurt. Some nights I don't get much sleep because the legs lock in spasms, and it is very painful. But if I give in and stay in bed, it would be easier the second day and much more easy the third and so on. When I get tired, I lose the vision in my right eye and the right leg drags a bit, but that just comes with the territory now. You learn to compensate and work around those things. Perhaps, in time, it will get better. Perhaps it will get worse. Whatever, I'm just grateful to be alive and doing as well as I am.

I have seen many of the things come true that Father sent me back to do. Yes, there are a few that haven't come about, and I'm still working on them. With time, patience, love, and faith, they will. After returning from beyond the veil, I've learned that impossible things just take a little longer.

Chapter Nineteen

Harry Finally Came to Take Her Home
by Alan Gomez, M.D.

During my monthly visits to the Convalescent Center in Provo, Utah, I became good friends to Grandma Rees. I came to look forward to our visits every month. I can't remember her full name. The last time I visited her in February, 1987, she was 102 years old.

Grandma Rees was from Richfield, and during our monthly visits, she would sit in her rocking chair humming tunes she had known during her life. When I spoke to her, she would carefully consider what I had said before answering. She was not senile.

Sometimes she would tell me about the exciting events in her life, like the first time a car drove through Richfield. She remembers the horses rearing up, and people saying it wouldn't last. The first train was the same way. The noise, black smoke, and cinders frightened the cattle and set some of the grain fields on fire. She remembered the first washing machine, the advent of indoor plumbing, the first airplanes, even the first man on the moon.

"The Lord better get me out of here," she would say. "I have seen enough." Then she would get very serious and begin talking about her husband, Harry, who had died 45 years earlier. She couldn't understand why he hadn't come to get her. She was afraid he didn't like her anymore or that he might have forgotten her.

One evening, upon entering the convalescent center, I noticed a dramatic change in Grandma Rees. I had never seen her so excited or so happy. She said Harry had visited her that morning, in her room.

"What time?" I asked.

"Oh early, about six," she said. Harry was a dairyman and liked to get an early start in the morning. She said he was still as handsome as ever, and still had his blond hair. She pointed to the southeast corner of the room where Harry had been standing.

I asked if she had touched him. She said she hadn't, that he had been standing in the air, tilting forward, like he was hanging from a string.

"What did he say to you?" I asked.

"He still loves me," she said, emotion in her voice. "He wants me to come with him." She was so excited, so happy. Finally, she knew that Harry still loved her.

"When is he coming for you?" I asked.

"In the morning, early," she responded, brightly. On the way out that night, I stopped to chat with Karen, one of the nurses. She had been talking with Grandma Rees earlier in the day and knew all about Harry's appearance. I asked Karen to call me at my office the next morning and let me know how Grandma Rees was getting along. Karen promised she would. In fact, she said she intended to come in early to check on Grandma Rees.

When Karen called over to my office the next morning, she reported that at 6:15 that morning she found Grandma Rees dead in her bed. Karen said there was a big smile on Grandma's face, and she was looking towards the southeast corner of the room. Harry had finally come to take her home.

About the Author

Lee Nelson is author of the best-selling *Storm Testament* series of historical novels and the new biographical novel on Porter Rockwell. Nelson is widely known for his authentic research—like killing a bull buffalo from the back of a galloping horse with a bow and arrow. Nelson's novels are widely syndicated, having appeared in serial form in over a hundred newspapers nationwide and in Canada.

Nelson's published books include eight historical novels and six non-fiction volumes. *Beyond the Veil* is Nelson's fourteenth book. His published magazine and newspaper articles number in the hundreds.

Nelson was born high in the Rocky Mountains in Logan, Utah, later graduating from high school in California. After studying at the University of California at Berkeley, he served a mission for the LDS Church in Southern Germany. Lee has a BA degree in English literature and an MBA degree, both from Brigham Young University.

Lee is a fulltime writer living on a small farm in central Utah with his wife Sharon and seven children.